CRIMINAL JUSTICE
PROFESSIONALS

PRACTICAL CAREER GUIDES
Series Editor: Kezia Endsley

CRIMINAL JUSTICE PROFESSIONALS

A Practical Career Guide

KEZIA ENDSLEY

ROWMAN & LITTLEFIELD
Lanham • Boulder • New York • London

Published by Rowman & Littlefield
An imprint of The Rowman & Littlefield Publishing Group, Inc.
4501 Forbes Boulevard, Suite 200, Lanham, Maryland 20706
www.rowman.com

6 Tinworth Street, London SE11 5AL, United Kingdom

British Library Cataloguing in Publication Information Available

Library of Congress Cataloging-in-Publication Data

Names: Endsley, Kezia, 1968- author.
Title: Criminal justice professionals : a practical career guide / Kezia Endsley.
Description: Lanham : Rowman & Littlefield, [2021] | Series: Practical career guides | Includes bibliographical references. | Summary: "Criminal Justice Professionals: A Practical Career Guide includes interviews with professionals in a field that has proven to be a stable, lucrative, and growing profession"—Provided by publisher.
Identifiers: LCCN 2020047799 (print) | LCCN 2020047800 (ebook) | ISBN 9781538145142 (paperback) | ISBN 9781538145159 (epub) Subjects: LCSH: Criminal justice, Administration of—Vocational guidance. | Criminal justice personnel. | Law enforcement—Vocational guidance.
Classification: LCC HV7419 .E54 2021 (print) | LCC HV7419 (ebook) | DDC 364.973023—dc23
LC record available at https://lccn.loc.gov/2020047799
LC ebook record available at https://lccn.loc.gov/2020047800

Contents

Introduction

Welcome to the Criminal Justice Profession

*W*elcome to a career in criminal justice! If you are interested in a career in this challenging, exciting, and rewarding field, you've come to the right book. This book is an ideal start for understanding the various careers available to you under the criminal justice umbrella. It discusses the paths you should consider following to ensure you have all the training, education, and experience needed to succeed in your future career goals.

As you might imagine, these are high-stress and high-reward professions. There is a lot of good news about these fields, and they are good career choices for anyone with a passion to help people. They are great careers for people who get energy from helping other people and can handle stress and pressure well. Demand for these jobs remains strong and the outlook is stable.

When considering any career, your goal should be to find your specific nexus of interest, passion, and job demand. Yes, it is important to consider job outlook and demand, educational requirements, and other such practical matters, but remember that you'll be spending a large portion of your life at whatever career you choose, so you should also find something that you enjoy doing and are passionate about.

So, what exactly do criminal justice professionals do on the job, day in and day out? What kinds of skills, educational background, and certifications do you need to succeed in these fields? How much can you expect to make, and what are the pros and cons of the various fields? Do career paths in criminal justice have a bright future? How do you avoid burnout and deal with stress and tragedy? Is this even the right career path for you? This book can help you answer these questions and more.

At its core, "criminal justice" can be described very simply as the system of law enforcement involving police, lawyers, courts, and corrections, used for all stages of criminal proceedings and punishment.[1]

A career in criminal justice spans from probation or parole officers to judges to resource safety officers working in schools. © SDI Productions/E+/Getty Images

The responsibilities and the career paths of a professional in criminal justice will vary greatly depending on which area within the profession they pursue. Therefore, this book offers a breakdown of the criminal justice system into its different professional areas.

Careers in Criminal Justice

A career in criminal justice is almost impossible to describe in just a few sentences because it can contain such a wide variety of roles, responsibilities, and locations. For the purposes of this book, we break these jobs into five main career paths, as follows (but keep in mind that you can ask five different people in the field about their career and you'll get five slightly different answers):

- *Police officers/detectives*: They can wear many hats during the course of a career. Their range of responsibilities will depend on the size of the department and on the population they serve, but often include patrolling areas for criminal activity and victim assistance, as well as investigating crimes and collecting evidence. Security officers in schools are trained police officers and spend much of their time interacting with and educating students about safety issues. They are also sometimes called *student/school resource officers* (SROs).

- *Parole/probation officers*: Sometimes called *correctional treatment specialists*, these officers work with and monitor offenders to prevent them from committing new crimes. They carry through with anything the court assigns to them, the most common being to supervise offenders and to investigate the offender's history (personal and criminal) before sentencing.[3] A parole officer supervises people who have been released from prison, whereas probation officers supervise people who have been placed on probation instead of serving jail time.
- *Correctional officers*: They work in local jails, state prisons, and federal penitentiaries. Correctional officers are the voice of authority and also ensure the safety and welfare of prisoners.[2]
- *Security guards/officers*: Security officers are usually officers of the law hired by a third party, such as a company or organization, to protect property and employees. They protect and enforce laws on an employer's property and may control access to authorized people only.
- *Criminal court prosecutors/judges*: A criminal prosecutor is a lawyer who works for the state to uphold the laws of the land. The role of a judge during a trial depends on whether a jury is present. In serious criminal cases, a jury is present and so the judge tries the facts. In other situations, it may be the judge's role to determine a verdict and assign punishment.

For these professions, this book covers the pros and cons, the educational/training requirements, projected annual wages, personality traits that match well, working conditions and expectations, and more. You'll even read some interviews from real professionals working in these fields. The goal is for you to learn enough about these professions to get a clear view of which one, if any, is a good fit for you. And, if you still have questions, we will point you to resources where you can learn even more.

Here are just a few characteristics of a career in criminal justice in general (we'll discuss career specifics in more detail in chapter 1):

- People skills—communication, empathy, understanding, sincerity, and friendliness—are very important in this field. You will work with many different kinds of people: people of all ages and ethnic backgrounds, with different past experiences with law enforcement, and with their own preconceived notions of your job. Many people might be fearful of you or your role in their life. Dealing effectively and positively with all kinds of people is a must.

- Good observation skills and a heightened sense of your surroundings are important. You need to be aware of what is going on all around you and develop a good sense as to whether people are telling the truth or lying to you.
- You need to be able to lead as well as work well in a team. Knowing when to lead and when to step back and give your charges a chance to make good decisions is sometimes difficult and something you will hone as you gain experience.
- Being physically fit is to your advantage when you work in most areas of criminal justice. It's a physically taxing field.

So, what are jobs in these areas like? Are jobs in one category only, or is there some overlap? What education, skills, and certifications do you need to succeed in these fields? What are the salary and job outlooks for each category? And what are the pros and cons of each area? This book answers these questions, and many more, in the following chapters.

> "Don't think because you aren't the smartest or whatever, that you can't do this job. You might still be the most qualified. Be who you are! Work hard, be humble, be persistent, and stay who you are. This can get you further than you can dream of."—Aleksandra Dimitrijevic, judge, Lake County Superior Court

The Criminal Justice Market Today

The United States Bureau of Labor Statistics forecasts that careers in the criminal justices fields are growing at the same rate or a bit slower than the average marketplace in the current decade (see https://www.bls.gov/emp/ for a full list of employment projections). The projected percent change in employment for

If you want to be able to help people during difficult times of their lives, criminal justice is a good field to consider. © wdstock/iStock/Getty Images

police officers in this country is 7 percent,[4] which is faster than the average growth rate for all jobs. For probation and parole officers, the projected percent change is 3 percent[5] and for security officers, job growth is about 4 percent.[6] For judges, projected percent change in employment is also 4 percent,[7] whereas for attorneys, the projected percent change in employment in 6 percent.[8] These jobs will always be necessary, which means you will have job security.

The demand for such jobs is affected by many factors in the United States:

- Demand varies depending on location and is driven largely by local and state budgets. If local and state governments experience budget deficits or are unable to increase their tax base, they may be unable to grow these departments as much as they would like. As a result, employment growth may be somewhat reduced in times of economic insecurity.
- There are relatively low rates of turnover in law enforcement, which makes the job market more competitive.
- On the other hand, there is a continuous need to replace workers who leave these occupations due to the high-stress nature and the physical demands of these jobs.

Chapter 1 covers lots more about the job prospects of these professions and breaks down the numbers for each one in more detail.

What Does This Book Cover?

This book takes you through the steps to see if a career in criminal justice might be right for you. It also gives you practical advice on how to pursue an education that will set you up to be a successful candidate for the type of job you might want.

- Chapter 1 describes the many specific paths that a career in criminal justice can take. From police officer to probation officer, corrections officer to judge, this chapter gives you an idea of the many different types of career options that exist.
- Chapter 2 describes the education requirements that you should know as you think about entering the criminal justice field. It talks about

steps that you can take as early as high school to prepare yourself, and it also describes the things you can do outside of class to be informed and ready.

- Chapter 3 looks at educational options that will lead you to a job in criminal justice. It discusses academic requirements, costs, and financial aid options that will help you understand your economic options.
- Chapter 4 helps you build the tools that will help you prepare for interviewing for jobs and internships. It also helps with cover letters, explains how to dress for meetings, and helps you understand what employers expect out of people looking for jobs.

Throughout each of the chapters, you'll read interviews with real people, at various stages of their careers, who chose some aspect of criminal justice as a career path. They offer real advice, encouragement, and ways to determine if this is something that might be right for you.

Where Do You Start?

You can approach this field in several different ways—whether you start immediately after high school or pursue a college degree first—depending on your long-term goals and interests.

Take a breath and jump right in to the next chapter. Chapter 1, "Why Choose a Career in Criminal Justice?," will answer lots of questions you might already have, including questions about job availability, salary, and whether your personality is built for a career in criminal justice. If you already know that this is the career path you want, it's still a good idea to read the chapter because it offers insight into specific pros and cons of this field that you might not have considered.

Regardless of your approach, it's important to understand that you will likely have to handle stressful, intense situations and will often be dealing with people during the worst times of their lives. Do you have—or can you develop—the mental toughness to deal with these kinds of situations with a level head on a daily basis? This is something important to consider as you find out more about careers in criminal justice.

Your future awaits! © tortoon/iStock/Getty Images

Even if you're not sure, keep reading because the next chapter is going to give you some really good information about your options in this field. It will break down the many different types of careers within criminal justice and will be helpful in determining which area you might find most interesting and rewarding.

Why Choose a Career in Criminal Justice?

You learned in the introduction that the professions in the criminal justice field—police officers, probation/parole officers, correctional officers, security guards/officers, and criminal court prosecutors/judges—are healthy and stable. You also learned a little bit about the demands and mental stresses of these professions. And you were reminded that it's important to pursue a career that you enjoy, are good at, and are passionate about. You will spend a lot of your life working; it makes sense to find something you enjoy doing, and of course, you want to make money and support yourself while doing it. If you love the idea of helping people for a living, you've come to the right book.

In this chapter, we break down these professions and cover the basics of each. The nice thing is that no matter what kind of training, postsecondary education, or degree you can/want to pursue, there is a way for you to work in criminal justice. College isn't for everybody. Not everyone wants to—or can afford to—spend four or more years at a university taking academic classes in order to find a good job.

Note: More than 50 percent of college students who start at a four-year institution drop out by year six of their college career.[1] An overwhelming majority of those students leave college with substantial student loan debt.

However, even though you might not need a college education, you do still need to finish high school, as well as pursue a technical degree and certifications, and maybe also attend academy. This training can take anywhere from six months to two years.

After reading this chapter, you should have a good understanding of each of these careers and can start to determine if one of them is a good fit for you. Let's start with the venerable police officer.

What Do Police Officers Do?

You probably don't need a career book to tell you what a police officer is. Police officers are ubiquitous in our country—every city, county, and state has a law enforcement department. But you may not realize how much police officers do in addition to day-to-day law enforcement.

A police officer can wear many hats during the course of his or her career. Your range of responsibilities will depend on the size of the department and on the population that you serve, but they often include the following:[2]

- Patrol areas for criminal activity and victim assistance
- Collect and secure evidence from crime scenes

Being a police officer can be extremely rewarding when you're able to help someone in real distress.
© KatarzynaBialasiewicz/iStock/Getty Images

- Conduct traffic stops and issue citations
- Observe the activities of suspects
- Respond to emergency and nonemergency calls
- Obtain warrants and arrest suspects
- Write detailed reports and fill out forms
- Prepare cases and testify in court
- Interact with the public in educational and nonenforcement capacities

Police officers can work in a variety of settings: local and state governments, the federal government, as detectives and criminal investigators, and even as fish and game wardens. Within every mid-sized and larger department there are officers who specialize in Special Weapons and Tactics (SWAT), vice, internal affairs, community outreach, the detective unit, education through Youth Explorer programs and camps, general patrol, and more. Each of these units is described in more detail here:

- Patrol unit: These officers are the most essential and basic part of the force, and they take up the majority of police time. These are the officers out on the beat, patrolling their assigned areas. They do traffic stops, check for warrants, and make arrests.
- SWAT unit: The SWAT team is an elite unit within a police force, used for exceptional crisis situations that require increased firepower or special tactics. They often deal with hostage and terrorist situations, for example.
- Vice unit: These officers focus on crime related to narcotics, alcohol, gambling, and prostitution. Sometimes these officers go "undercover" to investigate a potential illegal operation.
- Internal affairs unit: These officers investigate and unearth what really occurred when an officer or department is accused of misconduct. They typically work outside of the traditional command structure.
- Detective unit: These officers gather facts and collect evidence for criminal cases. They conduct interviews, examine records, observe the activities of suspects, and participate in raids and arrests. Detectives usually specialize in investigating one type of crime, such as homicide or fraud. They can be uniformed or plainclothes investigators.
- Community outreach and education unit: These officers work with and educate the community about local law enforcement by visiting schools,

giving tours, and holding and attending local events, with the goal of strengthening relationships with the community they serve. They engage with the community in nonenforcement, positive situations to strengthen relationships and trust within the community. *School safety officers* are actual police officers who work inside school buildings. They are responsible for all issues in schools that involve fights, drugs, gangs, and so on. If necessary, school safety officers can arrest students.

> "To be a resource officer in a school specifically, you need to be able to relate to the kids, be a good communicator, and be approachable. You can't take yourself too seriously—have fun with the kids. But you have to be honest with kids too. They don't want to hear a lot of fluff."—Sarah Livingston, master patrol officer and student resource officer

If you want to be a police officer or detective, you need at least a high school diploma or equivalent. In addition, many federal agencies and some local and state police departments require some college coursework or even a college degree. Many community colleges and four-year colleges and universities have programs in law enforcement and criminal justice, which can give you a leg up during the recruitment process.

Chapters 2 and 3 cover the educational and professional certification requirements in more detail.

THE PROS AND CONS OF BEING A POLICE OFFICER

The good news is that law enforcement is a stable and in-demand job. The job growth rate for law enforcement is on par with the national average, which you'll read more about in a following section. Partly due to the tarnished reputation of many police departments in recent years, the number of recruits entering general law enforcement is low all over the country right now, which means it's a good time to get into law enforcement if it's your calling.

As described previously, law enforcement includes many areas of specialization, which means you can find the area/unit that interests you the most, as well as move around during the span of your career for variety and interest. Camaraderie with other officers and with the department in general is also one pro that many in law enforcement state as a real benefit of the job. A real bond like a family develops over time with fellow officers. In addition, the pay and benefits are pretty good, especially when you consider it does not require an advanced degree. However, most police officers don't enter the profession for its job security or pay. They are drawn to law enforcement because they want to serve the public and help people.

Because you do not know what situations will be coming your way each day, the day-to-day environment/challenges can vary greatly. Being a police officer never gets mundane or boring. It's a new, exciting experience each shift. In addition, the twenty-four-hour shifts afford the officer multiple days off in a row and a flexible schedule during his or her off days.

Despite its many advantages, there are a few "cons" to consider as well. For one, it's a physically demanding job, and it can be stressful and dangerous. You could very well be put in harm's way. Officers can be injured when handling emergency situations. In addition, you will likely work weekends and holidays. Another drawback includes the amount of paperwork the job involves, which can be off-putting to some.

CAN YOU BE PART OF THE SOLUTION?

As a profession, law enforcement has suffered many public relations blows in the past years. Police officers are often seen as uncaring, racist, and jaded, and indeed, some of them are. This negative attention that law enforcement is getting from the media—that they are all racist and uncaring—has seriously curtailed the recruiting process. People see only the bad and not the good that police departments do every day.

This is greatly affecting how many young people want to go into law enforcement. Nationwide, this is a problem. There are tragically low numbers in police academies all over the country. But what you might not realize is that many departments are making a serious effort to confront and address these problems.

How do we fix community-police relations as a country? It's not something we can do in a year; it has to be forever. Young people who care about these issues, who have a passion to make things better, are the key to repairing and strengthening community relationships, which in turn will help with recruitment.

Are you one of those young people?

HOW HEALTHY IS THE JOB MARKET FOR LAW ENFORCEMENT?

The Bureau of Labor Statistics is part of the US Department of Labor (see https://www.bls.gov/ooh). It tracks statistical information about thousands of careers in the United States. For anyone wanting to become a police officer, the news is good. Employment is expected to grow 5 percent in the decade 2018 to 2028, which is as fast as the national average.[3] Demand is steady, yet the supply of recruits is at a national low, as mentioned in the sidebar "Can You Be Part of the Solution?"

These statistics show just how promising this career is now and in the foreseeable future:[4]

- *Education*: Requirements range from a high school diploma to a college degree. Check with your local and state agencies for their specific qualifications.
- *Training*: Recruits must graduate from their agency's training academy before completing a period of on-the-job training.
- *2019 median pay*: $65,170.
- *Job outlook 2018–2028*: 5 percent (as fast as the national average).
- *Work environment*: The majority (89 percent) work for state or local agencies, with another 7 percent working for federal agencies.

In addition to the training and education mentioned here, you usually must be at least twenty-one years of age, be a citizen of this country, and have no felonies. You must also meet stringent physical and personal qualifications. To increase your odds, be physically fit and have some postsecondary coursework in law enforcement or criminal justice.

FEDERAL LAW ENFORCEMENT OPTIONS

The federal government has created myriad agencies to help detect, investigate, prevent, and apprehend offenders who commit federal crimes. Due to the wide range of crimes under the federal umbrella, each agency has distinct and well-defined responsibilities. The requirements and qualifications for these agencies vary greatly. You can visit the following websites for more information if you're interested in any of these areas of federal law enforcement:

- Bureau of Alcohol, Tobacco, Firearms and Explosives (ATF): www.atf.gov
- Central Intelligence Agency (CIA): www.cia.gov
- Department of Homeland Security (DHS): www.us-immigration.com
- Drug Enforcement Administration (DEA): www.dea.gov
- Federal Air Marshal Agent (TSA): www.tsa.gov
- Federal Bureau of Investigations (FBI): www.fbi.gov
- Federal Emergency Management Agency (FEMA): www.fema.gov
- Internal Revenus Service Criminal Investigations (IRS-CI): www.irs.gov
- US Secret Service (USSS): www.secretservice.gov
- US Coast Guard Agency (USCG): www.uscg.mil

If you are interested specifically in federal law enforcement, there are many more agencies than those listed above. Start by searching the Internet and visiting the federal agency sites.

WOULD I BE A GOOD POLICE OFFICER?

Ask yourself these questions:

- Do I have a servant's heart: Am I driven to help and serve people?
- Can I keep my cool in stressful and traumatic situations?
- Am I physically fit or willing to get there? Do I enjoy working out and being active?
- Can I be compassionate, understanding, and nonjudgmental, no matter who I am treating?
- Do I have a sound, healthy mind and good coping skills?
- Am I a good communicator and ready and willing to communicate with all kinds of people?
- Am I a lifelong learner and excited at the prospect of continuously learning?

If the answer to any of these questions is an adamant "no," you might want to consider a different path. Remember that learning what you don't like can be just as important as figuring out what you do like. If you aren't sure if law enforcement is your gig but are still drawn to criminal justice, read on to learn about what it takes to be a probation or parole officer.

WHAT IS A MEDIAN INCOME?

Throughout your job search, you might hear the term "median income" used. What does it mean? Some people believe it's the same thing as "average income," but that's not correct. While the median income and average income might sometimes be similar, they are calculated in different ways.

The true definition of median income is the income at which half of the workers earn more than that income, and the other half of workers earn less. If this is complicated, think of it this way: Suppose there are five employees in a company, each with varying skills and experience. Here are their salaries:

- $42,500
- $48,250
- $51,600
- $63,120
- $86,325

What is the median income? In this case, the median income is $51,600, because of the five total positions listed, it is in the middle. Two salaries are higher than $51,600, and two are lower.

The "average income" is simply the total of all salaries divided by the number of total jobs. In this case, the average income is $58,359.

Why does this matter? The median income is a more accurate way to measure the various incomes in a set because it's less likely to be influenced by extremely high or low numbers in the total group of salaries. For example, in our example of five incomes, the highest income ($86,325) is much higher than the other incomes, and therefore it makes the average income ($58,359) well above most incomes in the group. Therefore, if you base your income expectations on the *average*, you'll likely be disappointed to eventually learn that most incomes are below it.

But if you look at median income, you'll always know that half the people are above it, and half are below it. That way, depending on your level of experience and training, you'll have a better estimate of where you'll end up on the salary spectrum.

What Do Probation/Parole Officers Do?

Probation/parole officers (also called *correctional treatment specialists*) oversee their assigned *probationers* (criminals who are allowed to stay out of prison if they do not commit another crime and follow particular rules) and/or *parolees* (criminals released from jail under certain legal conditions).[5] We'll discuss the difference between these two more fully in a bit.

In a nutshell, probation/parole officers make sure that the offender they are responsible for is following the conditions of their probation/parole. The duties of a parole/probation officer vary depending on the environment in which they work, but typically include the following:[6]

- Interview probationers and parolees, their acquaintances, and their relatives in an office or at a residence to assess progress
- Evaluate probationers and parolees to determine the best course of action for their rehabilitation
- Discuss and arrange treatment options
- Provide probationers and parolees with resources, such as job training
- Test for drugs and offer substance abuse counseling
- Ensure that probationers and parolees attend appointments, group programs, and other requirements as assigned by the court
- Perform prehearing investigations and testify in court regarding offenders' backgrounds
- Write reports and maintain case files on their offenders
- Report violations of probation and/or parole to the courts and to law enforcement

So, what is the difference between these two professions? Well, in some states, professionals perform the duties of both probation and parole officers. These jobs are more often separated by the kinds of offenders you work with, however. Probation officers, who are sometimes called *community supervision officers,* oversee offenders who have been given a sentence of probation instead of being sent to prison. Their job is to ensure that the probationer is not a danger to the community and help them rehabilitate through frequent visits with the probationer. Probation officers also write reports that describe the probationer's treatment plan and their progress since being on probation. Most work only with either adults or juveniles.[7]

Parole officers, on the other hand, work with people who have been released from prison and are serving *parole*, the goal of which is to help them reintegrate into society and be a productive and law-abiding member of it. Parole officers provide their parolees with information about various resources, such as substance abuse counseling or job training, to help them overcome their issues. The officers help to change the parolee's behavior and reduce the risk of that person committing another crime and having to return to prison.

Both probation and parole officers supervise probationers and parolees through personal contact with them and their friends and families (also known as *community supervision*). Probation and parole officers make regular contact with their parolees and probationers, by telephone and office visits, and they also check on them at their homes and places of work.

Note: A special kind of correctional officer, the *pretrial services officer*, looks into a pretrial defendant's background to determine if they can be safely allowed back into their community before their trial date. They must determine the risk and make a recommendation to a judge, who decides on appropriate sentencing (in settled cases with no trial) or the bond amount. When offenders are allowed back into the community, pretrial officers watch over them to make sure that they stay within the terms of their release and appear at their trials.[8]

When making home visits, probation and parole officers take into account the safety of the neighborhood in which the probationers and parolees live and any mental health considerations. Probation and parole officers also supervise drug testing and electronic monitoring of their charges.

THE PROS AND CONS OF BEING A PAROLE/PROBATION OFFICER

Being a probation officer can be a very rewarding job, when you are able to truly help someone reintegrate back into society. Probation/parole officers serve as role models and can provide career and life advice. You have the potential to make a real difference in a person's life, especially if you work with juveniles.

Correctional treatment specialists often meet with their charges before they are even released from jail. © South_agency/E+/Getty Images

You also get to tackle interesting problems and help your charges straighten out their lives. The job also has variety, and it allows you to help others while being out in society rather than being stuck behind a desk.

These roles are typically government jobs, which means good benefits that include insurance and pension plans. In addition, job security is good. Many offenders at the county and city level get probation for minor felonies, which means there will always be a longterm need for probation officers.

The drawbacks to being a probation/parole officer are several. It can be stressful and dangerous, especially for officers assigned to high-crime areas or to institutions/prisons. You may have to perform home and employment checks and property searches. Because of the hostile environments many encounter, some probation/parole officers carry a firearm or pepper spray for protection.

In addition, the offenders are sometimes hard to help and you will often fail. They may resent you and lie to you and otherwise make it hard for you to help them. You may also have to interact with people, such as family members and friends of your clients, who are upset, mistrusting, and otherwise difficult to work with.

Probation officers and correctional treatment specialists may have court deadlines imposed on them by the *statute of limitations*. The paperwork and caseload can be heavy at times, which means long hours.

HOW HEALTHY IS THE JOB MARKET?

The Bureau of Labor Statistics (see https://www.bls.gov) tracks statistical information about thousands of careers in the United States. According to their statistics, the US job market for probation and parole officers is expected to grow 3 percent in the decade from 2018 to 2028, which is a bit slower than average.[9]

These statistics give a snapshot of this career now and how it will look in the near future:[10]

- *Education*: A bachelor's degree in social work, criminal justice, behavioral sciences, or a related field is usually required, although this varies by jurisdiction.
- *2019 median pay*: $54,290.
- *Job outlook 2018–2028*: 3 percent (slower than average).
- *Work environment*: The majority work for county and state governmental court systems, jails, and parole offices. Some work for federal parole governmental bodies.

WOULD I MAKE A GOOD PAROLE/PROBATION OFFICER?

Ask yourself these questions:

- Can I keep my cool in stressful situations?
- Can I be compassionate, understanding, and nonjudgmental, no matter who I am treating?
- Do I have a sound, healthy mind and good coping skills?
- Do I have a servant's heart: Am I driven to help and serve people?
- Am I a good communicator and ready and willing to communicate with all kinds of people?

If the answer to any of these questions is an adamant "no," you might want to consider a different path. The nice thing is, if you feel driven to work in criminal justice in some capacity, there is a myriad of choices you can pick from.

LT. MAUREEN O'BRIEN:
BUILDING COMMUNITY RELATIONS FOR THE FUTURE

Maureen O'Brien. Courtesy of Maureen O'Brien.

Lt. Maureen O'Brien serves with the Community Engagement Unit for the Grand Rapids Police Department in Grand Rapids, Michigan. She has been a police officer for twenty-nine years for the city of Grand Rapids and has served many roles during her career, including working on patrol, vice, Internal Affairs, and mentoring youth through the Youth Police Explorer program since its inception in 2015.

Can you explain how you became interested in being a police officer?

In high school, my parents took my sister and me to Washington, DC. We toured the FBI headquarters, which piqued my interest in law enforcement. I was a competitive kid and enjoyed being active. I didn't think I would ever want to sit behind a desk. My oldest sister was engaged to a man going through the police academy about that time, and I would ask him many questions about the academy, and it furthered my interest in law enforcement. As I went to community college, I educated myself and looked into policing. I wanted to go to the federal level, but at that time, you needed to speak another language or have other aptitudes that I didn't have, so I opted to go into local law enforcement. It was that FBI tour that really opened my eyes to law enforcement as a career.

What are your main job duties?

I am currently the lieutenant of the Community Engagement Unit, with the responsibilities of hiring, recruiting, background investigations, the intern program, organizing, and staffing community events: our unit contains the public information officer, and the Boys and Girls Club officers.

We recruit for sworn police officers and our youth programs. We have the following youth programs: intern program, which is open to students enrolled in college; Police Explorer program, which is open to anyone age fourteen to twenty-one years of age; Youth Police Academy, which is a week-long academy for juniors and seniors in high school; the Chief's Advisory Board, which is open to youth in grades eight through twelve, and the on-base program for children ages nine to twelve.

Our unit participates in many recruiting events and community outreach, such as building tours (Boy Scouts and school groups) or visiting churches to talk to various immigrant populations to explain what we do, and to answer general questions. The goal of our community engagement is to strengthen relationships. We reach out to all types of communities. We go to block parties, festivals, career fairs, etc. We usually participate in more than 300 events a year.

We engage with the community in nonenforcement situations to strengthen relationships and trust within the community. We are constantly striving to have positive contacts with the community.

What is your formal educational background? Did your education prepare you for your job?

I went to a two-year college to obtain my associate's degree and then I transferred to Michigan State University, where I got a bachelor's in criminal justice.

I believe having some college experience helps you in many ways as a police officer. Our sponsored recruit position's minimum qualification is a GED or high school diploma. As an example, we had 570 people take our entry-level civil service exam for the sponsored recruit position, and 111 people failed it. On the other hand, the certified officers who take that exam, who must have, at minimum, two years of college to be in the academy, have a very low failure rate.

The college experience really helps with promotional exams too. These include scenario-based and written sections, with policy laws, local ordinances, etc. Having a formal education helps with these testing procedures, in my opinion, as college students are accustomed to preparing for and taking exams.

You do a lot of interviewing and writing in this job and college prepares one for these skill sets. People who write well generally go into our investigative units. Schooling can help you with listening and understanding skills and working in groups—these are all good in policing as well. College generally exposes students to different cultures and an open worldview, which is also helpful in this career as we interact with many different cultures and ethnicities in our city.

You learn to multitask in college, too, and you need that with the caseload on the force.

So, my education did prepare me as much as possible. However, the police academy and on-the-street learning is very educational.

What's the best part of being a police officer?

Currently, one thing for sure is working with our younger employees—the young officers and interns. You want to leave a legacy behind and be sure these employees are successful after you leave. Assisting them in acquiring the skills they need is very rewarding.

I enjoy not being behind a desk every day and being given various challenges weekly. I am constantly learning.

What is the most surprising thing about your job?

How many different hats I would end up wearing! You become proficient at many things. You might act as a type of social worker, psychologist, etc. It's different every day—all cases are different. This is challenging and keeps you sharp.

What are some things that are especially challenging? Anything especially challenging being a female on the force?

The hardest part is witnessing the suffering of people. Especially with children and other vulnerable people in the community. It's difficult to see it. You feel frustrated and helpless to remove them from inhumane environments.

In terms of being a female officer, it is a male-dominated career. I was an athlete and competitive growing up, so I was used to all that. But women can be too hard on themselves at times—don't second-guess yourself and your capabilities. Work hard. I am a big advocate of hard work. If you're not doing the work, you're not going to achieve your goals.

The guys are feeling the same worries and insecurities; they just might not vocalize it.

In 2013, I was promoted and back on patrol. I'd be out to dinner with a colleague, and a person in the community would walk up and thank the male officer for his service but ignore me. Your desire to serve must come from the heart, as you will not always be recognized for it, nor should you really expect it if you want a long career.

My advice to potential female officers: it's how you carry yourself and how you talk to people that will serve you well.

What are some characteristics of a good police officer? What people really don't fit well in law enforcement?

You must have a passion for this job. This is a calling—not really just a job. You must have a servant's heart or it won't work. If you love it, it won't feel like work.

The motivation must be to serve. Personal integrity—that must come from within.

Also, you need good interpersonal skills and the ability to listen. A full 98 percent of this job is communicating. That's with citizens, suspects, coworkers, and so on. It's essential.

What are some of the challenges facing law enforcement and the people in it?

For law enforcement in general, numbers of those pursuing this career are low nationally and every police department is hiring; it's a challenging time in law enforcement for staffing.

The negative attention that law enforcement is receiving from media—that all officers are racist and not caring—is really hurting recruiting. People tend to see only the bad officers that are being recognized in the media and not the thousands of good police officers and the work they do every day.

This is affecting how many young people want to pursue law enforcement. Nationwide, this is a real problem. There are tragically low numbers in academies all over the country. Then finding qualified candidates out of the low numbers can be challenging.

How do you fix community-police relations? That is something we are trying to do here. It's not something you do for a year—it's forever. I am optimistic that over the coming years our community relationships will be strengthened, which in turn will help recruitment.

What advice do you have for young people considering a career in law enforcement?

The Golden Rule! It's important to treat everyone as you would want your mother or father to be treated. It becomes pretty easy if you live by that rule.

Develop a life outside of police work. Have friends outside of work. Maintain that balance. It opens you up and keeps you more balanced.

Have a passion for this job, but also work hard! I will take hard workers any day. You have to put in the hours. Have a passion for the people you serve.

Constantly learn—don't ever stop learning. Be open-minded so you'll be well-versed in many areas. Get proficient in many different areas, especially if you want to move up in leadership. It helps you a lot as a leader to have a variety of experiences.

How can a young person prepare for this career while in high school?

My biggest advice is to educate yourself. Do internships or go on ride-alongs. Try to get an accurate picture of the job—it's not like the shows on TV. Speak with police officers. Find a Police Explorer or volunteer program so you can be sure you are making the right decision. That way, you'll be knowledgeable about your decision sooner during the fact-finding process.

Be involved with community outreach and volunteer opportunities in the community. For one, this may give you a leg up in the hiring process.

Finally, make good decisions. We lose a lot of people through background investigations. Whether it is assaultive behavior, domestic situations, or certain misdemeanors, these can all rule you out. Patterns of bad behavior will certainly rule you out.

Any last thoughts?
It's a great career. It's been a journey and I've been blessed. I wish everyone who has an interest in this field and a genuine desire to help people would pursue it.

What Do Correctional Officers Do?

Correctional officers work in jails and prisons, watching over those who have been arrested and are waiting for their trial or who have been sentenced to serve time. They work in all kinds of correctional facilities, from local jails to federal correctional institutions. In a nutshell, their job is to keep the peace and keep the inmates, as well as themselves and other employees, safe.

Here are some of their standard day-to-day duties:[11]

- Make sure inmates follow the rules
- Keep order in the facility
- Supervise activities
- Inspect facilities regularly for security and safety issues
- Search inmates for contraband items, such as drugs or weapons
- Escort, transport, and maybe restrain inmates when they are going to court or medical facilities or are being transferred
- Write reports and fill out daily logs about inmate conduct and anything else of note that occurred during their shift

THE PROS AND CONS OF BEING A CORRECTIONAL OFFICER

The pros of being a correctional officer include a decent salary and good benefits, as well as job security. Besides their general pay, corrections officers usually enjoy state health benefits and can retire at the age of fifty, with twenty years of employment, or at any age, with twenty-five years of service.[12] State corrections officers receive adequate sick days and vacation time. The amount of time off that each corrections officer gets goes up with every year of service. There is also room for advancement as a correctional officer.

Many corrections departments give their correctional officers training based on the American Correctional Association Guidelines.[13] On-the-job training is likely, and you may also get firearms and self-defense training.

As with probation/parole officers, this job can be stressful and dangerous. Correctional officers have one of the highest rates of on-the-job injuries and illnesses, often due to clashes with inmates.[14] Because jail and prison security must be supplied 24-7, correctional officers work in shifts that cover all hours of the day and night, including weekends and holidays.

In addition, the job demands that officers be alert and ready to react throughout their entire shift, usually standing or walking for long hours at a time.

HOW HEALTHY IS THE JOB MARKET?

According to the Bureau of Labor Statistics, the US job market for correctional officers is expected to decline 7 percent in the decade from 2018 to 2028.[15] This is essentially because correctional officers are paid through state and local budgets, and many state governments have moved toward laws that shorten prison terms and provide other alternatives to prison, due to the high costs of keeping someone incarcerated. However, despite this decline in overall *existing* jobs, job prospects should still be good due to the need to replace officers who retire, transfer to other occupations, or leave the labor force.

These statistics give a snapshot of this career now and how it will look in the near future:[16]

- *Education*: A high school diploma or equivalent is required, with on-the-job training provided, including forearms and self-defense training
- *2019 median pay*: $45,300.
- *Job outlook 2018–2028*: -7 percent (declining).
- *Work environment*: The majority work for state or local correctional facilities and are therefor employed by state or local governments.

WOULD I MAKE A GOOD CORRECTIONAL OFFICER?

Ask yourself these questions, which are very similar to the questions for probation/parole officer:

- Can I keep my cool in stressful situations?
- Can I be compassionate, understanding, and nonjudgmental, no matter who I am dealing with?
- Do I have a sound, healthy mind and good coping skills?
- Do I have a servant's heart: Am I driven to help and serve people?
- Am I a good communicator and ready and willing to communicate with all kinds of people?
- Am I fit, strong, and confident in intimidating situations?

If the answer to any of these questions is an adamant "no," you might want to consider a different path. If you're a high school student and wondering if you are fit to be a correctional officer, take courses in criminal justice or psychology and try to visit your local jail. This can help you determine if this might be a good path for you.

SHANE VANNATTER: ROLE MODEL AND MENTOR

Shane VanNatter. Courtesy of Shane VanNatter.

Master Patrol Officer Shane VanNatter has been in the SRO Unit since 2009. He is a graduate of the National Association of School Resource Officers Advanced SRO class, an Advanced School Safety Specialist, and an ALICE (Alert-Lockdown-Barricade-Evaluate) instructor. Officer VanNatter has been a member of the CPD (Carmel Police Department) SWAT (Special Weapons and Tactics) team since 2010. He also serves as an advisor for the CPD Exploring Post for youth interested in law enforcement careers. In addition, he has been an instructor for the CPD Teen Academy since 2008. Officer VanNatter is a veteran of the United States Marine Corps and previously worked as a police officer in Logansport, Indiana, for seven years before joining CPD. He is married, has three adult children, and enjoys motorcycle riding, camping, and playing squash.

Can you explain how you became interested in being a resource officer?

After leaving my service in the United States Marine Corps, I was seeking a career that impacted lives. I was looking for another way to serve. When the opportunity arose to work as a school resource officer (SRO), I jumped at it. Often times in law enforcement it is hard to see positive results in your daily duties. As an SRO, I see the positive effect my job has in the faces and attitudes of the students, staff, and parents. I am often thanked for my work and I feel appreciated, which is rare for most police officers.

What is a typical day in your job?

One of the best parts of being an SRO is that there is no typical day. My day can start off with a chat with a student about his or her college plans and it can end with a counseling session with a student who's having an emotional crisis. Some days I'm forced to arrest students for possessing contraband, and other days I track down thieves who are breaking into student vehicles in the parking lot.

I frequently respond to assist staff members who teach our most emotionally and physically disabled students. When those students are having a bad day, it can be difficult for staff to manage alone. Many of our disabled students are in their early twenties and are big, strong young adults. Our large high school has over one thousand adult students in attendance each day! I spend a lot of time in the classroom. I teach a class on transition to college. I help students prepare for issues such as how to file a police report, what to do when you have a vehicle collision, how to avoid becoming a victim of crime, sexual assault prevention, applying the Indiana life-line law, and substance abuse counseling.

What's the best part of your job?

For me, the best part of my job is knowing my role keeps kids safe. Success begins with security. No student or staff member can focus or be successful if they don't feel safe in their environment. This could come from bullying, stalking, fighting, or a fear of an act of violence. Hopefully, my presence and education programs help people feel safe at school.

What's the most surprising thing about your job?

The long-lasting impact. I routinely have past students who text or email me with updates on their lives. I have a number of young men and women who joined the military or became police officers because of (at least partially) my presence in their lives. I often meet kids who don't have any direction or discipline. They want a role model. While I'm far from perfect, I do expect a lot from our students and give them a standard of conduct and character to live by.

What is your advice for young people thinking about a career in criminal justice (CJ)?

The CJ field is in dire need of smart, integrity-driven individuals. If a young person is interested in public service, one of the most important things they can do is to stay out of trouble. Nothing disqualifies more candidates than a history of drug use, alcohol offenses, or arrests. For any young person seeking a career in law enforcement (LE), I recommend they find a program like the Chicago Police Department (CPD) Teen Police Academy or Law Enforcement Exploring through the Learning for Life (LFL) program. These programs are essentially job-shadowing internships that expose youth to the LE field.

What Do Security Guards/Officers Do?

Security guards/officers patrol and protect property from illegal activity (such as theft or vandalism) as well as keep the people on said property safe. They work in a wide variety of places, including public buildings, retail stores and malls, airports, banks, parking lots, government buildings, and office buildings. Because many buildings are open twenty-four hours a day, security officers must often work around the clock. They must always remain alert and be on the lookout for anything unusual. Some security guards are armed.

Here are some of the things you may do as a security officer:[17]

- Enforce laws and protect property from theft and vandalism
- Monitor any alarms and closed-circuit TV (CCTV) cameras
- Respond to emergencies as needed and call for assistance from police, fire, or ambulance services when necessary
- Control building access to employees and legitimate visitors only
- Conduct security checks over a specified area
- Write reports on what you observe while on duty
- Detain violators

Recall that school safety officers are police officers who work inside school buildings. They are discussed within the police officer sections.

Being a security officer often involves monitoring CCTV and other surveillance efforts. © fatihhoca/ iStock/Getty Images

THE PROS AND CONS OF BEING A SECURITY GUARD/OFFICER

The good news is that the job outlook is strong, as more and more organizations prefer to have a security officer present on their property for safety. This job has variety too, and it's likely that every day will be different. This is especially true if you work at multiple sites or work at sites where you come across hundreds or thousands of people in a day. Security can be very interesting work. Security guards who work during the day may have a great deal of contact with other employees and the public, which can be fun and interesting.

You also get to see things and have access to areas most people never even dream of. Have you ever wanted a job where you get to go behind the scenes on a daily basis? Welcome to security.

To some extent, you can also find a schedule that works with your life. Security is needed 24 hours a day, 7 days a week, 365 days a year. That means the likelihood of finding a schedule that works for you is very good.

Now for the drawbacks. Most security guards spend considerable time on their feet, either at a single post or patrolling buildings and grounds. Some may sit for long periods behind a counter or in a guardhouse at the entrance to a gated facility or community.

The hours can be long and you might miss out on family events and holidays. This is especially true when you are low on the totem pole of seniority.

Finally, this job can potentially be dangerous, especially if you're working alone or in remote locations. This can include physical violence, such as being attacked. It can also include sexual harassment, bullying, and intimidation.[18]

HOW HEALTHY IS THE JOB MARKET?

Overall job opportunities for security guards are projected to be excellent by the US Bureau of Labor Statistics.[19] The sheer size of the occupation and the number of workers who leave the occupation each year typically means there are many job openings. Of course, there is always more competition for higher paying positions that require more training and experience.

These statistics give a snapshot of this career now and how it will look in the near future:[20]

- *Education*: A high school diploma or equivalent is required, with on-the-job training provided.
- *2019 median pay*: $29,710.
- *Job outlook 2018–2028*: 4 percent (as fast as average).
- *Work environment*: They work in a wide variety of places, including public buildings, retail stores, and office buildings.

WOULD I BE A GOOD SECURITY OFFICER?

Ask yourself these questions as a start:

- Can I keep my cool in stressful situations?
- Do I have a sound, healthy mind and good coping skills?
- Can I keep alert over many hours at a desk or on my feet?
- Am I a good communicator and ready and willing to communicate with all kinds of people?
- Am I fit, strong, and confident in intimidating situations?

If the answer to any of these questions is an adamant "no," you might want to consider a different path. There are many different paths in criminal justice, depending on where your interests lie.

What Do Criminal Court Judges Do?

In general, judges (who have law degrees and have been active members of the bar for at least five years) interpret the law in court by overseeing the legal process. They also conduct hearings and issue legal decisions. Note that criminal court judges work in state courts and most states use the election process to determine who serves as a criminal court judge. That means they must run for and win the position in their state.

Here are some of the things criminal court judges are responsible for:[21]

- Managing cases and setting trial schedules
- Hearing and ruling on motions
- Overseeing the jury-selection process
- Settling disputes between advocates
- Maintaining objective order between opposing attorneys
- Supporting witnesses
- Controlling sometimes contentious spectators
- In a "bench" trial, deciding whether the defendant is guilty or not guilty
- Determining and pronouncing penalties based on opposing attorney arguments (and jury recommendations)

THE PROS AND CONS OF BEING A CRIMINAL COURT JUDGE

There are many advantages to being a judge. Judges generally enjoy good hours, good pay, legal immunity for mistakes, large research and support resources and staff to help them, professional esteem, job security, and relatively early retirement with a good pension.

The disadvantages include stress and responsibility. The work may be stressful, as judges sometimes work with difficult or confrontational individuals. The stakes are very high as well, as you may be determining a person's fate, perhaps even whether they live or die, if your state accepts the death penalty as legal (thirty states do).[22] The barrier to entry is also very high, as you need a law degree (that's seven years of postsecondary schooling) and you'll need to run for the office in your state.

In addition, the rules of conduct are much stricter than for lawyers, in general, because judges are held to much higher standards. You must convey a "proper" and upright image, which limits your public behavior, including the way you dress, the way you talk and act, the places you go, your social life, and sometimes even your personal life. As a judge, you are considered a pillar of the community and your behavior is scrutinized accordingly.

HOW HEALTHY IS THE JOB MARKET?

It's certainly true that judges play a critical role in the legal system, and their services will continue to be needed into the future. However, budgetary cuts in federal, state, and local governments may prevent empty judge positions from being filled or new ones from being created. If there are budget cuts, this could limit the employment opportunities of judges working for local, state, and federal government agencies.

The prestige associated with becoming a criminal court judge, and the fact that they need to be elected into the position, ensures that there will be stiff competition for these positions. Most job openings come about when a judge is leaving the occupation to retire, to teach, or because their elected term is over.

Criminal court judges earn a good living but have considerable responsibility in affecting people's lives. © dcdebs/iStock/Getty Images

These statistics give a snapshot of this career now and how it will look in the near future:[23]

- *Education*: Doctoral or professional law degree.
- *2019 median pay*: $120,090.
- *Job outlook 2018–2028*: 3 percent (slower than average).
- *Work environment*: All judges and hearing officers are employed by the federal government or by local and state governments. Most work in courts.

WOULD I BE A GOOD CRIMINAL COURT JUDGE?

First consider whether you are willing to attend college and law school, a total of seven years of postsecondary schooling. If that sounds like something you don't mind doing, consider these other qualities needed to be a good judge:

- Am I patient, open-minded, understanding, and compassionate? (You need to be able to deal with people calmly and hear and consider the views of all sides of a case.)
- Can I learn and apply complicated legal rules and procedures to different facts and circumstances?
- Can I learn new concepts and ideas quickly?
- Am I honest and ethical?
- Do I have a sound, healthy mind and good coping skills?
- Can I avoid being influenced by identity, race, gender, political status, wealth, or relationship of the party or lawyer and make sound decisions?
- I am a lifelong learner? (Continuing legal education programs are very important in remaining current in the law.)
- Can I communicate well with people of all backgrounds, ages, and circumstances? Can I express myself clearly, concisely, and grammatically, orally and in writing? (This includes the ability to listen.)

If the answer to any of these questions is an adamant "no," you might want to consider a different path. Being a judge is a big commitment that starts with law school, after college. Do your research about the law and law schools to see if this is truly something that you're drawn to.

Summary

In this chapter you learned a lot about the different careers under the "criminal justice" umbrella: police officers, probation/parole officers, security officers, and criminal court judges. You learned about what people in these professions do in their day-to-day work, the environments where you can find these people working, some pros and cons about each career path, the median salaries of these jobs, and the outlook in the future for all these careers. Hopefully, you even contemplated some questions about whether your personal likes, career goals, and preferences meld well with these callings. At this time, you should have a good idea of what each job looks like. Are you starting to get excited about one career choice over another? If not, that's okay, there's still time.

An important takeaway from this chapter is that no matter which of these professions you might pursue, a real desire to help people should be at the forefront of your mind if you want to be successful in any criminal justice field. The risks, stresses, and challenges of these professions won't likely be worth it to you if you aren't ultimately driven to help people. You need a "servant's heart," as they say, to excel in this career choice.

In chapter 2, we dive into forming a plan for your future. We cover everything there is to know about educational requirements, certifications, training courses, and more, for each of these careers. You'll learn about finding summer jobs and making the most of volunteer work as well. The goal is for you to set yourself apart—and above—the rest.

2

Forming a Career Plan in Criminal Justice

Now that you have some idea what criminal justice careers are all about—and maybe you even know what you are interested in—it's time to formulate a career plan. For you organized folks out there, this can be a helpful and energizing process. If you're not a naturally organized person, or if, perhaps, the idea of looking ahead and building a plan to adulthood scares you, you are not alone. That's what this chapter is for.

After we talk about ways to develop a career plan (there is more than one way to do this!), we will dive into the various requirements. Finally, we will look at how you can gain experience in the field through explorer programs, camps, shadowing, ride-alongs, certifications, and more. Yes, experience will look good on your resume and in some cases it's even required. But even more important, getting out there and seeing what criminal justice professionals do, day-to-day, is the best way to determine if it's really something that you'd enjoy. When you find a career that you truly enjoy and have a passion for, it will rarely feel like work at all.

If you still aren't sure if a career in criminal justice is right for you, try a self-assessment questionnaire or a career aptitude test. There are many good ones on the web. As an example, the career-resource website monster.com includes its favorite, free self-assessment tools at https://www.monster.com/career-advice/article/best-free-career-assessment-tools. The Princeton Review also has a very good aptitude test geared toward high schoolers at https://www.princetonreview.com/quiz/career-quiz.

This chapter could just as well have been titled "How to Not End Up Miserable at Work." Because really, what all this is about is achieving happiness. After all, unless you're independently wealthy, you're going to have to work.

That's just a given. If you work for eight hours a day, starting at eighteen years old and retiring at sixty-five, you're going to spend around 100,000 hours at work. That's about eleven years. Your life will be much, *much* better if you find a way to spend that time doing something you enjoy, that your personality is suited for, and that your skills help you become good at. Plenty of people don't get to do that, and you can often see it in their faces as you go about your day interacting with other people who are working. In all likelihood, they did not plan their careers very well and just fell into a random series of jobs that were available.

> **Tip:** The whole point of career planning is not to overwhelm you with a seemingly huge endeavor, it's to maximize happiness. Your ultimate goal should be to match your personal interests/goals with your preparation plan for college/careers. Practice articulating your plans and goals to others. When you feel comfortable doing this, you have a good grasp of your goals and the plan to reach them.

PLANNING THE PLAN

You are on a fact-finding mission of sorts. A career fact-finding plan, no matter what the field, should include these main steps:

- Take some time to consider and jot down your interests and personality traits. Are you a people person or do you get energy from being alone? Are you creative or analytical? Are you outgoing or shy? Are you organized or creative, or a little of both? Take a career-counseling questionnaire (found online or in your guidance counselor's office) to find out more. Consider whether your personal likes and preferences meld well with the positions you are considering.
- This time, think about how you've done at school and how things have worked out at any temporary or part-time jobs you've had so far. What are you really good at, in your opinion? And what have other people told you you're good at? What are you not very good at right now but would like to become better at? What are you not very good at and are okay with not getting better at?

YOUR PASSIONS, ABILITIES, AND INTERESTS: IN JOB FORM!

Now forget about work for a minute. In fact, forget about needing to ever have a job again. You won the lottery—congratulations. Now answer these questions: What are your favorite three ways of spending your time? For each one of those things, can you describe why you think you, in particular, are attracted to it? If you could get up tomorrow and do anything you wanted all day long, what would it be? These questions can be fun but can also lead you to your true passions. The next step is to find the job that sparks your passions.

Take out your list of traits and look it over. Pretend you're not you. Instead, you're a hiring manager at a company. What kind of job might be good for the person who wrote what you're reading? Do they sound like someone who would work well with others? Do you think they would work better on their own, or helping out on a team? For example, if you wrote down a sport as a favorite thing to do, was it something like tennis, swimming, or wrestling? If so, it may be that you prefer to achieve things more on your own, on your own terms. If you wrote down football, basketball, softball, or volleyball, it could be that you're more comfortable working together with others to achieve a common goal.

Now it's time to do fact-finding from the job's perspective:

- Find out as much as you can about the day-to-day of criminal justice professionals. In what kinds of environments do they work? Who do they work with? How demanding is the job? What are the challenges? Chapter 1 of this book is designed to help you in this regard.
- Find out about educational requirements and schooling and certification expectations. Will you be able to meet any rigorous requirements? Chapter 3 will help you understand the educational paths and certification requirements.
- Seek out opportunities to volunteer or shadow those doing the job. Use your critical thinking skills to ask questions and consider whether this is the right environment for you.

Part of finding the right career for you is striving for a good work-life balance as well. © marekuliasz/
iStock/Getty Images

- Build a timetable for taking required certifications and exams, such
  as the Scholastic Aptitude Test (SAT) and the American College Test
  (ACT), applying to schools, visiting schools, and making your decision.
  You should write down all important deadlines and have them at the
  ready when you need them.
- Continue to look for employment that matters during your college
  years—internships and work experiences that help you build hands-on
  experience in and knowledge about your actual career.

"The criminal justice field is in dire need of smart, integrity-driven individuals. If you
are interested in public service, one of the most important things you can do is to
stay out of trouble. Nothing disqualifies more candidates than a history of drug use,
alcohol offenses, or arrests."— Shane VanNatter, master patrol officer and student
resource officer

- Find a mentor who is currently working in your field of interest. This
  person can be a great source of information, education, and connections.

A mentor can help you in many ways. © Chris Ryan/iStock/Getty Images

Don't expect a job (at least not at first); just build a relationship with someone who wants to pass along their wisdom and experience. Coffee meetings or even emails are a great way to start.

WHERE TO GO FOR HELP

If you aren't sure where to start, your local library, school library, and guidance counselor's office are great places to begin. Search your local or school library for resources about finding a career path and finding the right schooling that fits your needs and budget. Make an appointment with a counselor or send an email to ask about taking career interest questionnaires. With a little prodding, you'll be directed to lots of good information online and elsewhere. You can start your research with these four sites:

- The Bureau of Labor Statistics' Career Outlook site (https://www.bls .gov/careeroutlook/home.htm). The US Department of Labor's Bureau of Labor Statistics site doesn't just track job statistics, as you learned in chapter 1. There is an entire portion of this site dedicated to young adults looking to uncover their interests and match those interests with jobs currently in the market. There is a section called "Career Planning for High Schoolers" that you should check out. Information is updated based on career trends and jobs in demand, so you'll get practical information as well.

- The Mapping Your Future site (https://www.mappingyourfuture.org/) helps you determine a career path and then helps you map out a plan to reach those goals. It includes tips on preparing for college, paying for college, job hunting, resume writing, and more.

- The Education Planner site (http://www.educationplanner.org) has separate sections for students, parents, and counselors. It breaks down the task of planning your career goals into simple, easy-to-understand steps. You can find personality assessments, get tips for preparing for school, learn from some Q&As from counselors, download and use a planner worksheet, read about how to finance your education, and more.

- TeenLife (https://www.teenlife.com/) calls itself "the leading source for college preparation" and it includes lots of information about summer programs, gap year programs, community service, and more. They believe that spending time "in the world" outside of the classroom can help students do better in school, find a better fit in terms of career, and even interview better with colleges. This site contains lots of links to volunteer and summer programs.

- The Princeton Review has a different online quiz (www.princetonreview .com/quiz/career-quiz). It has twenty-four questions, each one comparing two professions and you choose the profession you would rather be in, assuming both pay the same salary. You see the results when you're done.

- Ask to talk to a high school guidance counselor about criminal justice careers. They are likely to be able to offer you lots of information about local explorer programs, possible ride-along opportunities, camps, and other career opportunities.

- If you're still really confused and feel like you're no closer to knowing what you want to do, you may want to consult with a career coach or personal coach to help you refine your understanding of your goals and how to pursue them. These professionals specialize in figuring out what sorts of careers and jobs may be apt for different people.

- Conduct "interviews" with people working in any jobs in your community that you are considering. Feel free to ask them anything—what they enjoy about their work, what they find the most challenging, how they entered the field, advice on getting started, whether they would be willing to help you or provide a recommendation, and so on. You may even be able to visit them at their workplace and see firsthand what's involved. How do you find these people? Start asking around. You can ask your parents, your parents' friends, your teachers, and your school's guidance counselors. You could also do an online search with your hometown and job title as keywords.
- Use these sites as jumping-off points and don't be afraid to reach out to a real person, such as a guidance counselor or your favorite teacher if you're feeling overwhelmed.

WHAT IF I DROPPED OUT OF HIGH SCHOOL?

In many ads for jobs you'll see something like "high school diploma or equivalent required." What does "equivalent" mean? Well, it means you passed the General Educational Development (GED) exam. Once you earn that credential, you can use it like a high school diploma to pursue further technical or vocational (or college) education and apply for jobs.

In most states you must be at least sixteen years old to sit for the GED exam (in some states it's eighteen). The exam covers four topic areas: math, language arts, science, and social studies. The GED exam is now only administered on computer, so you need to at least know how to work a mouse and keyboard. Settle in, because completing the test usually takes all day.

You can register for the GED exam at www.ged.com. This website will also tell you everything you need to know about taking the exam, including when and where you can take it and any fees you'll need to pay.

MAKING HIGH SCHOOL COUNT

Regardless of the career you choose, there are some basic yet important things you can do while in high school to position yourself in the most advantageous way. Remember, it's not just about having the best application; it's also about figuring out which areas of criminal justice you would actually enjoy and which ones don't suit you.

- Use the summers to get as much experience as you can. Explorer programs, summer camps, and ride-alongs are all options you can find if you do enough digging. Volunteer in as many settings as you can.
- Hone your communication skills in English, speech, and debate. You'll need them to speak with everyone, such as patients, criminals, and fellow employees.
- Learn first aid and CPR. You'll need these important skills regardless of your profession.
- You will almost certainly need more training beyond your high school courses, but high school is the best place to learn the basics of many skills that are put to use in criminal justice. The following are some high school courses that can be of great benefit to anyone seeking work in criminal justice:

  ○ *Psychology/Sociology*: Learning about the human mind and the motivations of individuals, abnormal and otherwise, is good base knowledge to have if you plan on working in criminal justice. Psychology provides insights into why people do what they do and what their behavior says about them—you can rest assured that this comes in handy in the criminal justice profession.

  ○ *English/Language Arts/Communication*: The better you can communicate with others, the more efficient and effective you will be on the job. This is something employers truly value. And that's not just true for verbal skills. Being able to communicate accurate, complex medical information clearly to offenders and their family members is an important component of success.

  ○ *Foreign Languages*: You can have a real leg up on job prospects if you know the language used by offenders and clients that you'll interact with, not to mention you'll be able to break down the barrier of language to reach people in times of stress. If Spanish is common in your area, for example, beef up on those Spanish classes.

  ○ *Social Studies*: You may not see right away why studying history, political science, or government would be necessary to work as a correctional officer. But the fact is, to get along smoothly in the modern workplace you need to know some background on your own culture and its institutions. Employers want their employees to be well-rounded and knowledgeable and to be able to carry on conversations with people from different backgrounds. For example, history tells us why things are the way they are and where these things came from. All of this knowledge makes you a more well-rounded individual who can interact with the public in meaningful and positive ways.

ALEKSANDRA DIMITRIJEVIC: IT'S ALL ABOUT LISTENING

Aleksandra Dimitrijevic. Courtesy of Aleksandra Dimitrijevic.

Aleksandra Dimitrijevic has served in a variety of positions at the Lake County, Indiana, Prosecutor's Office for more than fifteen years, including as a violent crimes prosecuting attorney. She earned her undergraduate degree from Boston University in 1959 and her law degree from Indiana University McKinney School of Law in 2000. She was admitted to the Indiana Bar in 2003 and is currently judge of the Lake County Superior Court.

Can you talk about your education, background, and experience?

After high school in Indiana, I wanted to leave and go out east. I was interested in journalism and ended up at Boston University, in their college of communication. I took a film class and then wanted to be a film editor. I loved college in general, and my dad told me to think about law school. My dad is an immigrant from the former Yugoslavia and he had to flee out of his country for safety reasons. He worried about me going to Los Angeles (for the film industry). I worked for a Chicago production company for a while and didn't like it. So, I went to law school at Indiana University in Indianapolis. The first year was awful! It was so hard. I was lucky to have opportunities in clerkships, and I worked in the prosecutor's office in violent crime. That piqued my interest.

Can you explain how you became interested in being a judge? Why a criminal court judge?

My mother read a lot to me as a child. Mysteries such as Nancy Drew. I loved solving crimes. Even when I was thinking about journalism, I liked the investigative part. I gravitated toward criminal cases; they are much more interesting, more in the field. When I did apply to the prosecutor's office, I truly did love the felony side. I started in traffic court and made my way up through the system. My goal was to get into the felony division. It was exciting. The police would solve the crime and the prosecutor would have to put it together in a story and show who and why. Your job was to convince. When you win a case, if you can give a family closure or relief, well that means something, and that feels good. I did that for sixteen years. When the judicial seat became available, I wanted to try for it. I had a lot of empathy and I wanted to help people. I thought I could make more of an impact if I were a judge.

I was appointed by the Indiana governor in February 2019. I took the bench in March.

What's a "typical" day in your job?

I say good morning to everyone when I arrive. Most of my work comes to me electronically, but sometimes there are actual physical papers to sign. I get a report about who is in custody, then I take the bench. Court starts at 8:45 a.m. on a criminal day. I read them their rights. I then call them up for cases, one by one. If they have an attorney, the issue will get resolved through plea agreements and such. The goal is always to get people back on track.

Afternoon court begins at 1:00 p.m. These are repeat offenders, driving with a suspended license, and so on. They can't pay their tickets. We have specific calls that deal with these kinds of issues. We save Thursday afternoons for trials and typically have about eighty defendants.

If I am not on the bench, I am doing research for rulings. I read case law statutes, write opinions, read attorneys' e-files, and approve/deny motions. I spend a lot of time on specialized driving privileges (for offenders who have a suspended license but need permission to drive to work, for example).

We also have night court on Wednesday nights—these are people contesting traffic tickets, etc.

On civil court days, we see fewer cases because they are more time consuming. We see about forty people. We handle most of the cases that come through—this is the majority of our caseload. These aren't usually violent people; they are just off track. It's a high-volume court but they aren't violent crimes.

What's the greatest challenge facing people working in the criminal justice system at this time?

In my area of work, there are so many people with some type of addiction. We try to help them but they can't get past it. They keep coming back. A lot of these people are poor, don't have great home lives, and struggle with substance abuse. They might want to better themselves but don't know how to do it. We try to give them resources to get things back on track. They often don't have a support system at home. We often see the same people again and again. And that's frustrating. How can you help people with substance and mental issues? It's a serious challenge.

What's the best part of being in this field?

When I can help a defendant, and they tell me that I motivated them to make changes and they feel like I helped them turn things around. I don't judge them in a bad way. It's normal to struggle. When they come back and thank me for helping them and appreciate my perspective, that's meaningful.

What's the most challenging part of being a judge?

I thought I would do all these things—drug programs, etc. Problem-solving courts. It's harder than I thought. When you call as a judge, people do respond faster. I thought that would help me get things done quicker. But the red tape is so involved and it's such a process. It was eye opening because it takes so much jumping through hoops.

I thought I would be more biased against defendants, but I wasn't. I wasn't pro state and I saw that I was able to handle it. It's a very lonely job. Judges are isolated. You can't hang out with the attorneys or the police anymore. When people talk to me, both sides have to be there. I am now isolating. I cannot go to political functions and I can't endorse anyone. People treat you really well or they stay away from you.

Do you think your education adequately prepared you for your job?

Yes and no. Any education that forces you to discuss a topic will prepare you for this. Law school didn't necessarily teach me the jobs I have done. Law school taught me to rid myself of my ego—they belittled me and made me realize I really didn't know much. Then I had to really figure out a problem. I had to be able to argue my perspective and back it up and explain why.

You have to have good communication skills. It's about listening and talking to people. That's the bottom line.

Where do you see the field of criminal justice going in the future?

The trend across the country is creating problem-solving courts. Not punishment, rehabilitation. A problem-solving-court judge has a limited role. The prosecutor drives the court. In those cases, offenders are required to do something, like go to therapy, classes, etc., and if they meet the stipulations, the case against them will be dismissed. This is the trend across the country. "Three strikes you're out" is going away. Drug-related cases, especially, are going this way. It's becoming more about plea agreements than trails and jail time.

I've had people send me letters from jail who have been incarcerated for thirty years for a drug case. Prosecutor must agree to it. It's hard to get these people out— the verdict stands. It was wrong, but we couldn't always change it. People have to appeal to us and we look at the case. It's on an individual basis.

What traits or skills make for a good judge?

You need to be a good communicator. You have to like to read and be well-read. You have to control your temper and be open-minded to all types of people. Attorneys talk a lot. Let them talk. You have to listen well. Listen to all of it before you actually make up your mind. Don't prejudge. The staff might get impatient about people blathering on, but people just want to get stuff off their chest. They just want a chance to say what is on their mind.

What advice do you have for young people considering this career?

Being a lawyer is an honorable profession. On the prosecution side, you don't make a ton of money. You are a public servant. I love it. You need to want to help people. I feel honored that I was given this opportunity by the governor to be a judge. You fight for people, for victims, as a prosecutor. You are there for someone else. You see the worst in people. Being a judge has been an amazing experience because you can impact how people live and help them get on with their lives and be better. It's impactful. It's not about money.

How can a young person prepare for a career in criminal justice while in high school?

You don't have to study criminal justice or anything law related to go to law school. You have to make good grades. You *can* study criminal justice, but you don't have to. If you want to be an investigator, crime-scene investigators are police officers. Crime labs are chemistry and bio graduates. It's a lot of work. Talk to people who are in the field to see what it's like. Any degree you pursue can help you get into law school. For example, I studied film!

Any closing comments?

Don't think because you aren't the smartest or whatever, that you can't do this job. You might still be the most qualified. Be who you are. My family background told a special story about me and I embraced that. Work hard, be humble, be persistent, and stay who you are. This can get you further than you can dream of.

EDUCATIONAL REQUIREMENTS

The educational and certification requirements for criminal justice professionals differ widely across these varied fields, and also differ depending on where you plan on serving. The nice thing is that, with a few exceptions, you can enter a criminal justice profession at many different levels and with very little postsecondary education experience. Security guards and correctional officers can be hired directly out of high school, often with little or no experience, and can then be trained completely by their employer and third parties.

Police officers also often enter their respective academies directly from high school, although many pursue bachelor's degrees in criminal justice and other related concentrations before entering the force. This is something to consider especially if you want to become a detective down the line. Also, probation/parole officers are usually required to have a bachelor's degree in criminal justice or a related field.

Lawyers/prosecutors, as mentioned in chapter 1, need a law degree (JD). In addition, to be a judge, you need several years of experience serving as a lawyer. The following sections cover all the traditional requirements in more detail, and then cover a few exceptions as well.

EDUCATIONAL REQUIREMENTS FOR SECURITY OFFICERS

In order to be a security officer, you'll need a high school diploma or equivalent (GED). That said, candidates with associate's degrees (two-year college degrees) have a leg up and are typically hired in more desirable positions.[1]

You will most likely need to pass psychological screening tests that show you are stable and of sound mind, and have a clean background check. Employers will look at your criminal background of course, but might also review motor vehicle records and credit reports.

Some level of on-the-job training is provided, depending on where and for whom you work. This might include firearms and self-defense training. If you want a leg up in the field, people who have experience with video surveillance equipment have better job prospects, and those with a background in law enforcement also have an advantage.[2]

EDUCATIONAL REQUIREMENTS FOR CORRECTIONAL OFFICERS

As mentioned in chapter 1, correctional officers are typically required to have high school diploma or equivalent. Of course, having an associate's degree in criminal justice or a similar field can give you a leg up and help with promotions and upward mobility.

Just as with security officers, you will likely be required to go through a background check that includes criminal and motor vehicle records. You may also need to pass psychological screening tests that show you are stable and of sound mind.

Many corrections departments give their correctional officers training based on the American Correctional Association Guidelines.[3] You can likely expect on-the-job training and may also get firearms and self-defense training.

EDUCATIONAL REQUIREMENTS FOR PROBATION/PAROLE OFFICERS

Probation/parole officers typically need a bachelor's degree in social work, criminal justice, or behavioral sciences, although this varies depending on where you work. Some states allow you to become a probation officer while in the last semester of your degree program.

Many parole and probation officers, especially at the federal level, have master's degrees in criminal justice. In addition to their training, federal officers must have at least two years of work experience.[4]

You can get experience working in the court system or interning at a probation office. In many agencies, age and experience are equal to higher education. Be sure to check with your local and state agencies for their specific qualifications.

EDUCATIONAL REQUIREMENTS FOR POLICE OFFICERS

If you want to be a police officer, you need at least a high school diploma or equivalent. In addition, many federal agencies and some local and state police departments require some college coursework or even a college degree. Many community colleges, four-year colleges, and universities have programs in law enforcement and criminal justice, which can give you an advantage during the recruitment process. Again, check with your local and state agencies for their specific qualifications.

You will be expected to pass written, physical, and medical examinations prior to being considered for a job opening. Here, too, is where some formal postsecondary education can really help. Being able to write well and take tests well can make a difference.

"Having some college experience helps you in many ways as a police officer. As an example, we had 570 people take our entry-level civil service exam, and 111 people failed it. On the other hand, the certified officers who take that exam, who must have at the minimum two years of college to be in the academy, have a very, very low failure rate. College experience really helps with the promotional exams too. These include scenario-based and written sections, with policy laws, local ordinances, etc. Having a formal education helps with all these tests. You do a lot of interviewing and writing and college helps with this too."—Maureen O'Brien, twenty-nine-year veteran police officer

Once you are hired as a new recruit, you must graduate from the agency's training academy before completing a period of on-the-job training, a process similar to firefighters. These academy programs usually take about five months to complete. These programs and their qualifications are discussed in more depth in chapter 3.

In addition to the training and education mentioned here, you usually must be at least twenty-one years of age (in a few places you can be as young as eighteen), be a citizen of this country, and have no felonies. You must also meet stringent physical and personal qualifications.

Firearms training is part of police training academy. © RichLegg/E+/Getty Images

EDUCATIONAL REQUIREMENTS FOR PROSECUTORS AND JUDGES

As mentioned in chapter 1, in order to be a prosecutor or serve as a judge in any capacity, you must first obtain a law degree. This is formally called the juris doctor degree (JD), also known as the doctor of jurisprudence degree, and it's the graduate-entry professional degree in law (you begin law school after receiving a bachelor's degree). Most law schools offer only a traditional three-year program. However, there are a few accelerated JD programs (two years) and part-time programs (usually completed in four years) available in limited areas.

After receiving your law degree, you must pass "the bar" in your state. If you want to be considered eligible for a term as a judge, you typically have to practice law for a minimum of five years. Recall from chapter 1 that criminal court judges work in state courts and most states use the election process to determine who serves as a criminal court judge. That means you must run for and win the position in your state.

If you are serious about attending law school, a bachelor's degrees in history, business, English, political science, economics, arts and humanities, or psychology are all viable paths to entering law school. Your grades must be excellent and you'll need to do well on the Law School Admission Test (LSAT) to be accepted into law school. For more information about the LSAT and choosing a school, see www.lsac.org.

> **Note:** A *bar association* is a professional group of qualified lawyers (collectively known as "the bar," or "members of the bar"). The word *bar* comes from the old English/European custom of using an actual railing to separate the area where court business was done from the viewing area for the general public. In the United States, it's the American Bar Association (ABA). Check out their website: www.americanbar.org.

NETWORKING

There's an old saying: "It's not what you know, it's who you know." And actually, in many cases, it's really who *they* know. *Networking* means cultivating a web of relationships and using those relationships to make new ones. The connections and affiliations between people and groups of people make up what's called a *social* network. Social networking is powerful and has become very

Networking with others is a great way to make contacts and find mentors. © PeopleImages/E+/Getty Images

important in the modern workplace. About 85 percent of jobs/opportunities are found through personal contacts.[5]

THE CONCEPT OF SOCIAL NETWORKING

Imagine you have ten contacts in your social network. You could represent yourself as a dot in the middle, and your ten contacts as ten dots arranged in a circle around you. Then you could draw a line connecting you to each of them, like spokes on a bike wheel. Now imagine that each of *them* knows ten people. Draw ten dots in a circle around each of those dots and lines connecting those original ten dots out to their new dots. And of course, each of those *new* dots would also have ten dots, and so on.

What happened here, and what does it mean? It means your original ten contacts could potentially introduce you to one hundred new contacts. And *those* contacts could then introduce you to one thousand *new* contacts. As you can see, this simple concept swiftly starts adding up to big numbers. In fact, you would only have to go through three more rounds of drawing dots and you would be looking at more than a million people. And this example is conservative. Ten is a pretty small number to start with. You probably know a lot more than ten people, and each of them surely does too.

That should give you a sense of the tremendous power of networking and why it's a major force in the business world. You can use networking as part of your work, and you can use it to find work. For example, all the criminal justice professionals interviewed for this book were found through the author's social network.

Tip: LinkedIn (www.linkedin.com) is a professional networking website specifically designed as a tool for cultivating business contacts. You can sign up for a free account by going to the website and clicking the "Sign Up" button. Once you're signed up, you start adding your own connections. The more, the better. You can search the site for positions and job titles, and LinkedIn will show you job openings and potential contacts who are contacts of *your* contacts. In this way, you can grow your number of professional contacts very quickly.

HOW TO NETWORK

Let's go back to the beginning, to those first ten dots you imagined drawing. Who are they? You are likely a young person without a lot of experience or contacts in the career field you may be interested in. How can you possibly network your way into a job in that field from where you are now?

Well, take a minute to really consider all the people you know. To begin with, you can probably count some or all of the following among your contacts right now:

- Parents
- Extended family members (aunts and uncles, cousins, perhaps grandparents)
- Friends (plus their parents and older siblings)
- Social media friends (Instagram, Snapchat, Twitter, Facebook, and so on)
- Teachers
- School administrators
- Coaches, club leaders, and sponsors (band, student council, yearbook)
- Clergy (pastor, rabbi, imam, priest)
- Employers and former employers
- Coworkers and former coworkers
- Neighbors
- Fellow church or club members (people you know from church or local clubs like 4-H, Lion's Club, Elks and Moose lodges, or Knights of Columbus)

Suddenly it seems that you actually know quite a few people. Now, imagine how many people *they* know.

Tip: Don't forget that your high school guidance counselor can be a great source of information and connections as well.

You probably have an address book of some kind. If not, you can pick one up at a local drug store or grocery. Start writing down your contacts' names, phone numbers, and email addresses, drawing from the preceding bulleted list. In many cases, you may only have a person's name. That's okay for now: write the name down, too. These single names can serve as placeholders until you get their phone numbers and email addresses.

Once you have a good number of contacts written down, come up with a short statement that says what kind of help you're looking for. For example, something like this:

> Hi, _____. I'm looking for contacts in the _____ field as I consider my career choices. I am wondering if you might know someone I could talk to about this, to expand my network as I look for training and job opportunities. If you know of anyone who might be of help and you feel comfortable passing along their contact info, I would truly appreciate it!

Save your statement in generic form and then paste it into emails, instant messages, or text messages, and customize it as appropriate each time (*don't* forget to customize it). If you prefer speaking on the phone, prepare a similar brief appeal that you can deliver verbally. Be brief, but don't be shy. Most people are more than willing to help if they can. Try to contact five people per day. That's enough to start making progress expanding your network, but it's not enough to be overwhelming or burdensome. In no time, your address book will be filling up. For example, by the end of the first week you will have contacted thirty-five people and may have collected some thirty-five new contacts.

Once you've made a new contact, use a similar script or speech with them, being sure to mention your common acquaintance by name. See if they are available to meet to discuss the career, training, and job opportunities you're interested in. If your meeting goes well, don't hesitate to ask if they know of someone else you may want to talk to.

Follow these important but simple rules for the best results when networking:

- Do your homework about a potential contact, connection, school, or employer before you make contact. Be sure to have a general understanding of what they do and why, but don't be a know-it-all. Be open and ready to ask good questions.

- Be considerate of professionals' time and resources. Think about what they can get from you in return for mentoring or helping you.
- Speak and write with proper English. Proofread all your letters, emails, and texts. Think about how you will be perceived at all times.
- Always stay positive.
- Show your passion for the subject matter.

Summary

In this chapter you learned even more about what it's like to be a criminal justice professional and how you might have a path to get where you want to go. This chapter discussed the educational requirements of the different areas of criminal justice, from high school diplomas to college degrees to doctorate degrees. Are you starting to picture your career plan? If not, that's okay, there's still time.

In chapter 3, we go into a lot more detail about pursuing the best educational path. The chapter covers how to find the best value for your education. It includes discussion about financial aid and scholarships. By the end of chapter 3 you should have a much clearer view of the educational landscape and how and where you fit in.

3

Pursuing the Education Path

*I*f you've decided that you want to further pursue a career in criminal justice, it's time to start looking at the best way to make that happen. Should you pursue a bachelor's or associate's degree? Should you take a certification course in law enforcement? When it comes time to start looking at colleges or post-secondary (after high school) schools, many high schoolers tend to freeze up at the enormity of the job ahead of them. This chapter will help break down this process for you so it won't seem so daunting.

Yes, finding the right learning institution is important, and it's a big step toward you achieving your career goals and dreams. The last chapter covered the various educational requirements of these professions, which means you should now be ready to find the right institution of learning. This process should also be about finding the right fit so that you can have the best possible experience during your post high school years.

> "Choose your career for the right reasons. Make sure it's a good fit for you and your personality. You should find joy in it or don't do it!"—Matthew Broadnax, master patrol officer and student resource officer

Attending postsecondary schooling isn't just about completing the program requirements, getting certified, or even getting an associate's degree. It's also about learning how to be an adult, managing your life and your responsibilities, being exposed to new experiences, growing as a person, and otherwise becoming someone who contributes to society.

US News & World Report puts it best when they say the education that fits you best is one that will do all these things:[1]

Community colleges, as long as they are accredited, can be great places of learning for a fraction of the cost. © Hispanolistic/E+/Getty Images

- Offer a degree that matches your interests and needs
- Provide a style of instruction that matches the way you like to learn
- Provide a level of academic rigor to match your aptitude and preparation
- Offer a community that feels like home to you
- Value you for what you do well

Note: According to the National Center for Educational Statistics (NCES), which is part of the US Department of Education, six years after entering college for an undergraduate degree, only 59 percent of students have graduated. Barely half of those students will graduate from college in their lifetime.[2]

PREPARING AND EDUCATING YOURSELF WITHOUT A COLLEGE DEGREE

This section is relevant to those interested in security officer, correctional officer, and police officer positions. To be a probation/parole officer, you will very likely need a bachelor's degree, and to be a prosecutor or judge, you will need a JD (law degree).

So, to be a police officer, you can apply to many law enforcement departments with simply a high school degree. You usually have to be twenty-one to be eligible, although in some places, it's eighteen. If you are certain you want to be a police officer and you either have a "shoe in" to a department or are fortunate to be applying when the numbers are low, this can be a successful way to enter the field. In addition to starting your career as soon as you're eligible, the benefits are that the department will usually pay for your certifications and you'll be working (and earning a paycheck) as you are being trained and certified.

> "If a man empties his purse into his head no one can take it away from him. An investment in knowledge always pays the best interest."—Benjamin Franklin (attributed)[3]

However, having some postsecondary education experience can benefit you in many tangible and intangible ways as a police officer. You will be expected to pass written, physical, and medical examinations prior to being considered for a job opening. In addition, officers have to be able to write and communicate as a daily part of their jobs. They write up reports that are read by other officers, judges, and others who were not on the scene and are expected to be able to communicate the incident fully to all parties. Being able to write well and take tests well is an important part of being promoted within the department, and having at least some formal postsecondary education can help in this regard.

Remember that many federal agencies and some local and state police departments require college coursework or even a college degree. Be sure to check with your local and state agencies for their specific qualifications.

Note: According to Discover Policing, a website managed by the International Association of Chiefs of Police (IACP), "You cannot go wrong with more education. Most departments, regardless of their requirements, give higher pay to recruits with four-year degrees."[4]

Once you are hired as a new recruit, you must graduate from the agency's training academy before completing a period of on-the-job training. These academy programs usually take three to eight months to complete and include classroom coursework covering legal studies, interpersonal studies, writing classes, and stress management, among others. The physical training portion— or skills development—usually involves defensive tactics certification, driver training, firearms qualifications, and more. The academy prepares you for the police force you will be assigned to when you graduate.

> **Tip:** Many community colleges, four-year colleges, and universities have programs in law enforcement and criminal justice. The website www.criminaljusticedegree schools.com provides a good overview of the kinds of degrees and classes you might want to consider. You can also visit www.discoverpolicing.org for a great overview of policing.

Security and correctional officers can also enter the field directly from high school. You typically must be at least twenty-one and a US citizen. An associate's degree (a two-year degree) in criminal justice or something similar can set you apart from the crowd. The federal prison system, where the jobs are more handsomely paid, requires correctional officers to have a bachelor's degree, be between twenty-one and thirty-seven years old, and have at least three years experience supervising or counseling inmates.[5]

SARAH LIVINGSTON: A RESOURCE FOR STUDENTS

Master Patrol Officer Sarah Livingston has been with the Carmel Police Department in Carmel, Indiana since 2004. She is a 2004 graduate of Purdue University with a degree in law and society and a minor in psychology. (Boiler Up!) Prior to being assigned to the Student Resource Officer (SRO) Unit in 2007, Officer Livingston was a detective in the Criminal Investigations Divisions for Carmel, focusing on crimes against children. She served in criminal investigations for six years.

Sarah Livingston. Courtesy of Sarah Livingston.

Can you explain how you became interested in being a police officer? And why an officer in an educational setting?

Originally, I was in investigations—specifically dealing with crimes against children. I thought there was a greater need to be proactive to prevent crimes against children—help in these situations before the police ever got involved. I wanted to help kids understand it's okay to come to officers with their problems.

My actual goal in joining the police department was simply to help kids. When I joined in 2010, I was assigned to children. I really liked it, although the cases could be very intense at times. I wanted to get ahead of it, so to speak, which is why the role of SRO appealed to me.

What's a "typical" day in your job?

There is no real typical day. I start at middle school to welcome kids entering the building. It's all up for grabs—some days I teach elementary kids about body safety, communication, drugs, respect, and so on. Sometimes I respond to behavioral complaints and try to mentor and help those students who are struggling. Sometimes I train with the police department: this could be firearms training or emergency vehicles training, for example. Sometimes I do home welfare checks on students when we haven't heard from them in a few days and there are no calls from the parents.

I'm in charge of four total schools. The issues I deal with are hardly ever criminal—it's more about mentoring, teaching about good choices, and helping steer the kids to better behavior.

What's the greatest challenge facing people working with juveniles in the justice system at this time?

The hardest thing is keeping up with all the social media. The amount of time kids spend doing all that and the culture behind the screen is a real challenge. Kids put so much weight into other people's opinions of them, even online. They take to heart what people say and it can be hurtful. It's an added pressure for them to be in the loop at all times. It takes a toll mentally and emotionally.

What's the best part of being in this field?

The kids! You could be having a really bad day, but knowing that you've connected with someone and made them feel safe is the best. Kids who actually come to me for help. . . . Making a difference in their lives is really the best, hands down.

What's the most challenging part of being a resource officer?

Being too emotionally attached to some of the kids and wanting to help them as much as you can, but knowing you can only do so much. They have to deal with it, or their family does.

Do you think your time at the academy adequately prepared you for your job?

Yes, I think there is always room for more education. My degree at Purdue and the academy both really help. There is also so much more learning and training to be done as you work in the job. There is constant training, such as firearms training (which is twice a year). Carmel prides itself on having the most educated police officers. We learn about defensive tactics, emergency vehicle operation, active-shooter drills, ethics training, and other kinds of specialized training. SROs also attend several conferences a year that are related to school safety.

Where do you see the field of criminal justice going in the future?

I have been with the department for sixteen years and we are bigger and busier than we ever were. The calls for service are more severe than when I started. But we are also more equipped and have more manpower than before. It's hard to say where we will be in the future. Our town just passed a referendum to have police officers in every school—and that effort will build up over several years.

What traits or skills make for a good SRO?

To be a resource officer in a school, specifically, you need to be able to relate to the kids, be a good communicator, and be approachable. You can't take yourself too seriously—have fun with the kids. But you have to be honest with kids, too. They don't want to hear a lot of fluff.

It's just as important to deal well with teachers and parents. I am a resource to them too. I encourage my admins and teachers to contact me for help. I can help them find the answer they need. I am there for them too.

What advice do you have for young people considering this career?

If this is the career that you want, keep in mind the reason you are doing it. You'll get praise one day, but the next, you'll be criticized. If you want to help keep people safe, don't forget that's why you are doing it. It's not for the accolades.

How can a young person prepare for a career in criminal justice while in high school?

We have a summer program called the Teen Academy. They get to go to a mini boot camp and see what it's like: classes, fitness, firearms, defensive tactics, tour the jail, etc. Students get to interact with police officers on a more personal basis. Many forces have Citizens' Academy too. In addition, take criminal justice and law classes in college. Look for doing a ride-along with your police department. Also look for Police Explorer programs. Ours, which accepts kids ages fourteen to twenty, helps with traffic control. There are a lot of ways you can get a feel for the career and see what officers really do, day in and day out.

FOR THOSE PURSUING A HIGHER-ED DEGREE

If you're currently in high school and are serious about attending college for a bachelor's or associate's degree before you begin your career, start by finding four to five schools in a realistic location (for you) that offer the degree/certificate/program in question. Not every school near you, or that you have an initial interest in, will offer the program you want, of course, so narrow your choices accordingly.

ALL ABOUT THE COMMON APP

The Common Application form is a single, detailed application form that is accepted by more than nine hundred colleges and universities in the United States. Instead of filling out a different application form for every school you want to apply to, you fill out one form and have it sent to all the schools you're interested in. The Common App itself is free, and most schools don't charge for submitting it.

If you don't want to use the Common App for some reason, most colleges will also let you apply with a form on their website. There are a few institutions that only want you to apply through their sites and other highly regarded institutions that only accept the Common App. Be sure you know what the schools you're interested in prefer.

The Common App's website (www.commonapp.org) has a lot of useful information, including tips for first-time applicants and for transfer students.

Consider attending a university in your resident state, if possible, which will save you lots of money if you attend a state school. Private institutions don't typically discount resident student tuition costs.

Be sure you research the basic grade point average (GPA) and Scholastic Aptitude Test (SAT) or American College Test (ACT) requirements of each school as well.

Note: For those of you applying to associate's or bachelor's degree programs, most advisors recommend that students take both the ACT and the SAT tests during their junior year (spring at the latest). You can retake these tests and use your highest score, so be sure to leave time to retake early senior year, if needed. You want your best score to be available to all the schools you're applying to by January of your senior year, which will also enable them to be considered with any scholarship applications. Keep in mind these are general timelines; be sure to check the exact deadlines and calendars of the schools to which you're applying!

Once you have found four to five schools in a realistic location for you that offer the degree/certificate in question, spend some time on their websites studying the requirements for admissions. Most universities will list the average stats for the last class accepted to the program. Important factors weighing on your decision of which schools to apply to should include whether or not you meet the requirements, your chances of getting in (but aim high!), tuition costs, availability of scholarships and grants, location, and the school's reputation and licensure/graduation rates.

WHAT'S THE DIFFERENCE BETWEEN VOCATIONAL SCHOOL AND COLLEGE?

They both provide postsecondary education, and they both award degrees, but there are some pretty big differences:

- Colleges and universities are designed for four-year bachelor's and graduate degree programs. Vocational schools are geared for two-year associate's degrees and various certificates for study lasting less than two years.

- In college, students take a wide variety of courses, some of which are outside their area of study. In vocational school, students study one subject with a narrow focus and an emphasis on practical training for a specific job. That's why it only takes two years instead of four.
- A large percentage of college students live on or very near campus. Most vocational students commute to class, and many hold down outside jobs.
- Colleges and universities cost significantly more to attend, often two or three times what vocational schools cost.
- At vocational schools, you won't see huge lecture halls filled with a couple hundred students taking notes on a lecture by a professor who doesn't know their names. Class sizes are usually small (twenty to thirty students) and often involve hands-on training in shops and labs.

The order of these characteristics will depend on your grades and test scores, your financial resources, and other personal factors. You, of course, want to find a school that has a good reputation, but it's also important to match your academic rigor and practical needs with the best school you can.

THE MOST PERSONAL OF PERSONAL STATEMENTS

The *personal statement* you include with your application to college is extremely important, especially when your GPA and SAT/ACT scores are on the border of what is typically accepted. Write something that is thoughtful and conveys your understanding of and passion for the profession you are interested in, as well as your desire to practice in this field. Why are you uniquely qualified? Why are you a good fit for this university? These essays should be highly personal (the "personal" in personal statement). Will the admissions professionals who read it, along with hundreds of others, come away with a snapshot of who you really are and what you are passionate about?

Look online for some examples of good ones, which will give you a feel for what works. Be sure to check your specific school for length guidelines, format requirements, and any other guidelines they expect you to follow.

And of course, be sure to proofread it several times and ask a professional (such as your school writing center or your local library services) to proofread it as well.

DAVID URBANSKI

Dave Urbanski received his undergraduate degree in economics from Wabash College and earned an MBA (Master of Business Adminstartion) from Loyola University in Chicago, in international business. He subsequently received his JD (law degree) from Valparaiso. He was a Lake County, Indiana, prosecutor for twenty years, handling felony criminal cases. He was a supervisor in one of the courtrooms and then became a homicide supervisor in Gary, Indiana, in the Lake County Metro Homicide Unit for several years. He currently works in Porter County as a felony deputy prosecutor.

Can you explain how you became interesting in being a deputy prosecutor?

In school I recognized that I enjoyed and was good at public speaking. On some level, I wondered how I could best take advantage of the skills I was good at. I liked trial work and being a lawyer. Trial work really interested me. Once I was in law school, I found that criminal cases were much more interesting to me. Civil work is fighting over other people's money, essentially, which did *not* excite me. Things flowed from there.

What's a "typical" day in your job?

Depends on what day it is. I have designated days for court calls. I'm in court in the morning with the judge. Multiple cases are called before the court—such as motions, suppression of evidence, no contest orders, and regular court jobs. It's about informing the court where you are in terms of where the case is going. This process consumes the morning.

On non-court days, I might gather evidence, hear verdicts, etc. Cases can mean one to two days in trial.

During a trial, we look over juries and give opening statements. The government moves forward with its evidence. There is a cross-examination by the defendants, bringing evidence to close, at which point the defendant can present his or her own evidence—rebuttal evidence only. Then there are the closing arguments. The government goes first and last (they have the burden of proof). Your closing argument may be limited to sixty minutes, and you can break that up in minutes before and after their closing argument. The government can rebut the arguments at the end.

On a normal workday, I have appointments with attorneys (pending cases resolutions and so on), depositions (using a court reporter and asking witnesses questions), and the defense attorney asking questions of your witnesses. I spend a great deal of time prepping cases: looking at what needs to be done to gather all the evidence; meeting with police officers; obtaining records; interviewing people; requesting lab tests for scientific testing; such as DNA, ballistics work, and fingerprints; and meeting with victims or their families to answer their questions.

Any given day can be vastly different. There is no real routine about it. You put out fires. Where I am now, it's Tuesday, Wednesday, and Thursday for trial. Scheduling is a big concern and an important component relative to the court schedule. You spend a lot of time working out scheduling matters.

What's the greatest challenge facing people working in the criminal justice system at this time?

The volume of activity versus the resources that are available is a real challenge. How many cases should one deputy have at one time? I have about 150 at one time. A Lake County deputy may have two hundred to three hundred he or she is are responsible for. It's all about putting out fires. Ninety percent plus end up in agreements because of this. We must have plea agreements or the system would come to a halt.

What's the best part of being in this field?

Trial work is the best! Preparing for trial and being in trial. Depending on the matter, it can be highly stressful and important, and it takes a toll. It takes months to prepare for a trial and it raises your stress level. Seeing the fruits of your labor in trial is very rewarding.

There is no better feeling in the world than getting a guilty verdict and providing justice for a family. It endorses your work as successful. Family members thank you and are grateful. It may have been a couple of years since the incident and the family has relief and justice now. That feels good.

What's the most challenging part of being a deputy prosecutor?

Time management is important. The volume of work and the limited resources to accomplish your work—including your own time—are constant challenges. Also, when you're dealing with fearful witnesses who live in the community where these events happened and they will be seen as the snitch on the block. You can't protect them.

Do you think your education adequately prepared you for your job?

Absolutely. All the way back to my undergraduate degree at Wabash. I undeniably received an education there. Thinking critically started there. That helped me move into the field of law for sure.

Where do you see the field of criminal justice going in the future?

The main thought now is "alternative sentencing." We have a clear and over-whelming problem with drug abuse—most of the activity in the criminal justice system is related to substance abuse. We are looking to provide assistance to those individuals rather than just punish them. Work release programs, problem-solving courts, mental health assistance, drug treatment, helping veterans who have crimes due to mental health issues. Don't burden people with felony criminal convictions that further prevent them from participating in society, getting jobs, etc. Expunged records even help people get jobs. This started in Indiana in 2014, when the criminal code was reformed because too many people were in prison. We are making an effort to incarcerate fewer and fewer people. Indiana prisons have filled up with drug dealers due to non-suspendible guidelines (also called "mandatory minimums"). Many offenders received a felony for drug dealing and have to be in there twenty years minimum (ends up being more like forty to fifty years). This is a problem countrywide.

The habitual enhancement penalties—"three strike rule"—where, if you commit a third felony, the penalty can be enhanced based on prior record. There used to be a thirty-year enhancement for that third felony—even if was a minor felony. This has now been recognized as unduly harsh. The enhancement is now two to six years for lower felonies.

Basically, we are looking to help people instead of just punishing them.

What traits or skills make for a good deputy prosecutor?

We have to embrace the fact that our job is to be a minister of justice. If you have a bad case, and the evidence is deficient, you have to know when to dismiss a case.

This is a good job for someone who isn't committed to always winning. One of the greatest mistakes I see with young lawyers is that think they have to obtain a conviction. The realty may be that there isn't probable cause. As you're moving through your case, you might find that witnesses lie and things fall apart. Recogniz-ing that you can't prosecute a case is also very important too. Can you prosecute the case or not?

Dismissing the charges is best in this case. Don't be afraid to see that a case isn't winnable. Maybe it didn't happen in the manner it was told. The whole system assumes presumption of innocence, so the burden is on the government to prove guilt.

What advice do you have for young people considering this career?

There is a volume of work you need to be ready for. Also, look at the financial circumstances—seven years of school is expensive and how will you pay for it?

Consider the income level versus the cost of your education. Just be aware and be realistic. Where does the job get you if you have $200,000–300,000 in student load debt? Some professionals are paying student loans up into their sixties.

How can a young person prepare for a career in criminal justice while in high school?

Chart out a path in terms of your work ethic, and a financial plan. Find internships and scholarships as much as you can. Recognize the schools you want to attend and utilize early programs and scholarships. Get in front of the ball. There are ever-rising costs. Your path of success is recognizing the point where it starts (in high school) and getting good grades so you can get grants and whatnot. It's a commitment that people need to understand sooner rather than later. There is a point of no return.

Any closing comments?

It is a wonderful profession. I've done many different jobs and worked with many different people. It's a job about relationships. That's the most important thing to take away if you're thinking about this field. It's always about establishing and maintaining relationships—with victims, police officers, lab personnel, etc.

CONSIDERING LAW SCHOOL

This section doesn't dive too deeply into the process of considering law school, because if you're reading this book, we assume that you have a way to go before you'll be ready to apply. Having said that, this section covers some basics that are good for you to know *now*, while you are still in the early stages of planning your future.

PICKING THE BEST SCHOOL

By "best," we don't just mean ones with great reputations, although that certainly helps. "Best" for you might mean an in-state school that is more reasonably priced, one that offers special programs or concentrations that interest you, or one that has accelerated options that meet your needs.

For example, accelerated, "3+3" programs allow students to earn both a bachelor's degree and juris doctor (JD) in six years. Typically, you'll study for three years, rather than four, at an undergraduate school and then spend what would normally be your senior year as a first-year law student. So, you get your undergraduate degree and your JD in six years instead of seven, saving both time and money.

Another thing to consider while looking for law schools is to consider where you'd like to practice law. As a law student, you'll get to be involved in the community through clinics and build connections with professors, which can help after law school if you stay and practice in that same area.

Ultimately, the same advice goes here as when picking colleges for your undergraduate study: match your interests to a school's strengths and opportunities, but keep cost in the forefront of your mind as well.

GETTING IN

The two most important pieces of your application are your undergraduate GPA and your Law School Admission Test (LSAT) score. In fact, some law school admissions departments openly claim that LSAT scores make up 70 percent of a student's admissions chances, with the other 30 percent dependent on your GPA.[6] So, how you score on the LSAT really matters. The good news is that you can take the LSAT up to three times a year if you want to maximize your chances. Schools take your highest score.

The LSAT is out of 180 points, and 150 is an average score. Few example, to get into a top-fourteen law school, you typically need to score above 162, and to get into a top-fifty law school, you need 154 or above.[7]

Be ambitious and apply to a few "reach" programs, but keep in mind the acceptance rates for each school, as well as the average LSAT scores and GPAs of their current classes. Be realistic with your expectations.

CONSIDERING THE COST TO BENEFIT RATIO

According to a report in 2020 by *US News & World Report*, the average annual cost of a public, out-of-state law school is $41,726, compared to a private school at $49,548 and public, in-state school at $28,264.[8] Keep in mind that's for one year of schooling. Even for the least expensive option—public, in-state school—the cost over three years is $84,792. Unless you are among the lucky few who have a trust fund or wealthy parents who will pay your way, that's a lot of debt to start a career with. So, how much will you make as an attorney, at least initially?

A 2020 survey by *US News & World Report* reported that, among the 181 ranked law schools that published the median private sector salary for their 2018 classes, the median salary was $75,000. Private practice salaries varied greatly, ranging from $50,000 to $190,000.[9]

The median starting salaries of JD graduates who entered the public sector in 2018 were much lower than those in the private sector. Among the 179 ranked law schools that reported this data, the median public sector salary was $58,000, with median salaries ranging from a low of $42,000 to a high of $74,000.[10]

This information isn't here to discourage you, but to give you a realistic idea of the debt-to-income ratio you'll be dealing with your initial years out of law school. The bottom line? If you're doing it for the money only, it's probably not worth it.

What's College Going to Cost You?

So, the bottom line: what will your undergraduate education end up costing you? Of course that depends on many factors, including the type and length of degree, whether the school is a private for-profit, private not-for-profit, or public institution, how much in scholarships or financial aid you're able to obtain, your family or personal income, and many other factors. The College Entrance Examination Board (www.collegeboard.org) tracks and summarizes financial data from colleges and universities all over the United States.

According to data reported to *US News & World Report* in an annual survey, the average cost of tuition and fees for the 2019–2020 school year at a four-year institution was $41,426 at private colleges, $11,260 for state residents at public colleges, and $27,120 for out-of-state students at state schools.[11]

Public two-year universities usually offer the most education value for your dollar. In 2018, according to the College Board, the average annual tuition at public two-year universities in the United States was $7,300.[12] But not all public universities will offer the program you're looking for. For vocational schools, average tuition depends greatly on where you live. In New Jersey, the average vocational school tuition is $9,167, and in New Mexico it's $3,125, for example.[13]

For information about law school costs, see the previous section dedicated to considering law school.

Note: According to the US Department of Education, as many as 32 percent of college students transfer between colleges during the course of their educational career.[14] This is to say that the decision you initially make is not set in stone. Do your best to make a good choice, but remember that you can change your mind, your major, and even your campus. Many students do it and go on to have great experiences and earn great degrees.

Costs go up every year. Generally speaking, there is about a 3 percent annual increase in tuition. In other words, if you are expecting to attend college two years after this data was collected, you need to add approximately 6 percent to these numbers. The good news is that financial aid and scholarships can offset tuition costs somewhat.

This chapter also covers finding the most affordable path to get the degree you want. Later in this chapter, you'll also learn how to prime the pumps and get as much money for your education as you can.

Tip: The actual, final price (or "net price") that you'll pay for a specific college is the difference between the published price (tuition and fees) to attend that college minus any grants, scholarships, and education tax benefits you receive. This difference can be significant. For example, in 2015–2016, the average published price of in-state tuition and fees for public four-year colleges was about $9,410. But the average net price of in-state tuition and fees for public four-year colleges was only about $3,980.[15]

WHAT IS A GAP YEAR?

Taking a year off between high school and college, often called a *gap year*, is normal, perfectly acceptable, or almost required in many countries around the world, and it is becoming increasingly acceptable in the United States. Even Malia Obama, former president Obama's daughter, did it. Because the cost of college has gone up dramatically, it literally pays for you to know, going in, what you want to study, and a gap year—well spent—can do lots to help you answer that question.

Some great ways to spend your gap year include joining the Peace Corps or AmeriCorps organization, enrolling in a mountaineering program or other gap-year-styled program, backpacking across Europe or other countries on the cheap (be safe and bring a friend), finding a volunteer organization that furthers a cause you believe in or that complements your career aspirations, joining a Road Scholar program (www .roadscholar.org), teach English in another country (https://www.gooverseas.com/blog/best-countries-for-seniors-to-teach-english-abroad for more information), or working and earning money for college.

Many students will find that they get much more out of college when they have a year to mature and experience the real world. The American Gap Year Association reports from their alumni surveys that students who take gap years show improved civic engagement, improved college graduation rates, and improved GPAs in college.[16]

See their website at https://gapyearassociation.org/ for lots of advice and resources if you're considering a potentially life-altering experience.

FINANCIAL AID AND STUDENT LOANS

Finding the money to attend college, whether for a two- or four-year degree, an online program, or a vocational-career college, can seem overwhelming. But you can do it if you have a plan before you actually start applying to college. If you get into your top choice, don't let the sticker cost turn you away. Financial aid can come from many different sources and it's available to cover all different kinds of costs you'll encounter while getting your education, including tuition, fees, books, housing, and food.

The good news is that universities often offer incentive or tuition discount aid to encourage students to attend. The market is often more competitive in favor of the student, and colleges and universities are responding by offering more generous aid packages to a wider range of students than they used to.

Here are some basic tips and pointers about the financial aid process:

- Apply for financial aid during your senior year. You must fill out the FAFSA (Free Application for Federal Student Aid) form, which can be filed starting October 1 of your senior year until June of the year you graduate.[17] Because the amount of available aid is limited, it's best to apply as soon as you possibly can. See fafsa.gov to get started.
- Wait until you receive all offers from your top schools and then use this information to negotiate with your top choice to see if they will match or beat the best aid package you received.
- To be eligible to keep and maintain your financial aid package, you must meet certain grade/GPA requirements. Be sure you are very clear on these academic expectations and keep up with them.
- You must reapply for federal aid every year.

Paying for your education can take a creative mix of grants, scholarships, and loans, but you can find your way with some help!. © designer491/iStock/Getty Images

Note: Watch out for scholarship scams. You should never be asked to pay to submit the FAFSA form ("free" is in its name) or be required to pay a lot to find appropriate aid and scholarships. These are free services. If an organization promises you you'll get aid or that you have to "act now or miss out," these are both warning signs of a less reputable organization.

Also, be careful with your personal information to avoid identity theft. Simple things like closing and exiting your browser after visiting sites where you entered personal information (like fafsa.gov) goes a long way. Don't share your student aid ID number with anyone either.

It's important to understand the different forms of financial aid that are available to you. That way you'll know how to apply for different kinds of aid and get the best financial-aid package that fits your needs and strengths. The two main categories that financial aid falls under are *gift aid,* which doesn't have to be repaid, and *self-help aid,* which is either loans that must be repaid or work-study funds that are earned. The next sections cover the various types of financial aid that fit in these areas.

NOT ALL FINANCIAL AID IS CREATED EQUAL

Educational institutions tend to define financial aid as any scholarship, grant, loan, or paid employment that assists students to pay their college expenses. Notice that "financial aid" covers both *money you have to pay back* and *money you don't have to pay back.* That's a big difference!

DO NOT HAVE TO BE REPAID

- Scholarships
- Grants
- Ferderal work-study

HAVE TO BE REPAID *WITH INTEREST*

- Federal government loans
- Private loans
- Institutional loans

SCHOLARSHIPS

Scholarships are merit-based aid that does not have to be paid back. They are typically awarded based on academic excellence or some other special talent, such as music or art. Scholarships can also be athletic based, minority based, aid for women, and so forth. These are typically not awarded by federal or state governments, but instead come from the specific school you applied to or private and nonprofit organizations.

Be sure to reach out directly to the financial aid officers of the schools you want to attend. These people are great contacts that can lead you to many more sources of scholarships and financial aid. Visit http://www.gocollege.com/financial-aid/scholarships/types/ for lots more information about how scholarships work.

GRANTS

Grants are typically awarded to students who have financial need, but can also be issued in the areas of athletics, academics, demographics, veteran support, and special talents. They do not have to be paid back. Grants can come from federal agencies, state agencies, specific universities, and private organizations. Most federal and state grants are based on financial need.

Examples of grants are the Pell Grant, the National Science and Mathematics Access to Retain Talent Grant (SMART), and the Federal Supplemental Educational Opportunity Grant (FSEOG). Visit the US Department of Education's Federal Student Aid site for lots of current information about grants (https://studentaid.ed.gov/types/grants-scholarships).

FEDERAL WORK-STUDY

The US Federal Work-Study program provides part-time jobs for undergraduate and graduate students with financial need so they can earn money to pay for educational expenses. The focus of such work is on community service work and work related to a student's course of study. Not all schools participate in this program, so be sure to check with the school financial aid office if this is something you are counting on. The sooner you apply, the more likely you will get the job you desire and be able to benefit from the program, as funds are limited. See https://studentaid.ed.gov/sa/types/work-study for more information about this opportunity.

LOANS

Many types of loans are available to students to pay for their postsecondary education. However, the important thing to remember here is that loans must be paid back, with interest. Be sure you understand the interest rate you will be charged. This is the extra cost of borrowing the money and is usually a percentage of the amount you borrow. Is the interest fixed or will it change over time? Is the loan and interest deferred until you graduate (meaning you don't have to begin paying it off until after you graduate)? Is the loan subsidized (meaning the federal government pays the interest until you graduate)? These are all points you need to be clear about before you sign on the dotted line.

There are many types of loans offered to students, including need-based loans, non-need-based loans, state loans, and private loans. Two very reputable federal loans are the Perkins Loan and the Direct Stafford Loan. For more information about student loans, start at https://bigfuture.collegeboard.org/pay-for-college/loans/types-of-college-loans.

MAKING HIGH SCHOOL COUNT

If you are still in high school or middle school, there are many things you can do now to help the postsecondary educational process go more smoothly. Consider these tips for your remaining years:

- Work on listening well and speaking and communicating clearly. Work on writing clearly and effectively.
- Learn how to learn. This means keeping an open mind, asking questions, asking for help when you need it, taking good notes, and doing your homework.
- Plan a daily homework schedule and keep up with it. Have a consistent, quiet place to study.
- Talk about your career interests with friends, family, and counselors. They may have connections to people in your community who you can shadow or will mentor you.

- Try new interests or activities, especially during your first two years of high school.
- Be involved in extracurricular activities that truly interest you and say something about who you are and want to be.

Kids are under so much pressure these days to "do it all," but you should think about working smarter rather than harder. If you are involved in things you enjoy, your educational load won't seem like such a burden. Be sure to take time for self-care, such as sleep, unscheduled down time, and other activities that you find fun and energizing. See chapter 4 for more ways to relieve and avoid stress.

Summary

This chapter dove right in and talked about all the aspects of postsecondary schooling that you'll want to consider as you move forward. Remember that finding the right fit is especially important, as it increases the chances that you'll stay in school and finish your degree or program, as well as have an amazing experience while you're there. The careers under the criminal justice umbrella have varying educational requirements, so finding the right educational fit can be very different depending on your career aspirations.

In this chapter, you learned about how to get the best education for the best deal. You also learned a little about how to write a unique personal statement that eloquently expresses your passions, how the SAT and ACT tests work, and scholarships and financial aid.

Use this chapter as a jumping-off point to dig deeper into your particular area of interest. Some tidbits of wisdom to leave you with:

- If you need to, take the SAT and ACT tests early in your junior year so you have time to take them again. Most schools automatically accept the highest scores.
- Make sure that the school you plan to attend has an accredited program in your field of study. Some professions follow national accreditation policies, while others are state-mandated and therefore differ across state lines. Do your research and understand the differences.

- Don't underestimate how important school visits are, especially in the pursuit of finding the right academic fit. Go prepared to ask questions not addressed on the school website or in the literature.
- Your personal statement is a very important piece of your application that can set you apart from others. Take the time and energy needed to make it unique and compelling.
- Don't assume you can't afford a school based on the "sticker price." Many schools offer great scholarships and aid to qualified students. It doesn't hurt to apply. This advice especially applies to minorities, veterans, and students with disabilities.
- Don't lose sight of the fact that it's important to pursue a career that you enjoy, are good at, and are passionate about. You'll be a happier person if you do so.

At this point, your career goals and aspirations should be gelling. At the least, you should have a plan for finding out more information. And don't forget about networking, which was covered in more detail in chapter 2. Remember to do the research about the school or degree program before you reach out and, especially, before you visit. Faculty and staff find students who ask challenging questions much more impressive than those who ask questions that can be answered by spending ten minutes on the school website.

In chapter 4, we will go into detail about the next steps: writing a resume and cover letter, interviewing well, follow-up communications, and more. This is information you can use to secure internships, volunteer positions, and summer jobs. It's not just for college grads. In fact, the sooner you can hone these communication skills, the better off you'll be in the professional world.

4

Writing Your Resume and Interviewing

N o matter which path you decide to take—whether you enter the workforce immediately after high school, go to college first and then find yourself looking for a job, or maybe doing something in between—having a well-written resume and impeccable interviewing skills will help you reach your ultimate goals. This chapter provides some helpful tips and advice on how to build a great resume and cover letter, how to interview well with all your prospective employers, and how to communicate effectively and professionally at all times.

The advice in this chapter isn't just for people entering the workforce full time either. It can help you score that internship, explorer program, or summer job, or help you give a great interview to impress the admissions office or local police station. The principles discussed here remain important throughout your working life, on and off the job. Learn them now, cultivate them as automatic habits, and they will serve you for as long as you're in the working world.

This chapter also has some tips for dealing successfully with stress, which is an inevitable byproduct of a busy life. Let's dive in.

FINDING AND APPLYING FOR THE JOB

To apply for a job you first have to know where to look for one. One of the quickest ways to find out what jobs are available in your field is to simply Google it (or search the Internet with whichever search engine you like best).

USING ONLINE JOB SITES

When companies and organizations want to hire new employees, they post job descriptions on job hunting or employee recruitment websites. These are a fantastic resource for you long before you're ready to actually apply for a job. You can read real job descriptions for real jobs and see what qualifications and experience are needed for the kinds of jobs you're interested in. You'll also get a good idea of the range of salaries and benefits that go with different types of criminal justice professions.

Pay attention to the "Required Qualifications," of course, but also pay attention to the "Desired Qualifications"—these are the ones you don't have to have, but if you have them, you'll have an edge over other potential applicants.

Here are a few sites to get you started:

- www.monster.com
- www.indeed.com
- www.ziprecruiter.com
- www.glassdoor.com
- www.simplyhired.com

USING PROFESSIONAL ORGANIZATIONS

One of the services provided by most professional organizations is a list of open positions. Employers post jobs here because organization members are often the most qualified and experienced. The further resources section in this book lists professional organizations for the different professions we've covered. Check online and talk to people in your field (such as your professors, neighbors, or local officers) to find out which organizations to join and where the best source of job information is likely to be.

NETWORKING

Some say the absolute best way to find a job is through networking. Your personal and professional contacts may know about an upcoming job that hasn't even been advertised yet. Sometimes an employer may even create a position for someone they want to hire. Keep in touch with the people you know in the field, at every level, and let them know that you're available.

Still wondering about how to network? Flip back to chapter 2 and check out the section aptly titled "Networking" for some useful tips.

CREATING A RESUME

If you're a teen writing a resume for your first job, you likely don't have a lot of work experience under your belt yet. Because of this limited work experience, you need to include classes and coursework that are related to the job you're seeking, as well as any school activities and volunteer experience you have. While you are writing your resume, you might discover some talents and recall some activities you did that you forgot about, which are still important to add. Think about volunteer work, side jobs you've held (baby sitting, volunteering in the courts, dog walking, etc.), and the like. A good approach at this point in your career is to build a functional resume, which focuses on your abilities rather than work experience, and it's discussed in detail next.

PARTS OF A RESUME

As mentioned, the functional resume is the best approach when you don't have a lot of pertinent work experience, as it is written to highlight your abilities rather than the experience. (The other, perhaps more common, type of resume is called the chronological resume and it lists a person's accomplishments in chronological order, most recent jobs listed first.) This section breaks down and discusses the functional resume in greater detail.

Here are the essential parts of your resume, listed from the top down:

- *Heading*: This should include your name, address, and contact information, including phone, email, and website, if you have one. This information is typically centered on the page.
- *Objective*: This is one sentence that tells that specific employer what kind of position you are seeking. These should be modified to be specific to each potential employer.
- *Education*: Always list your most recent school or program first. Include date of completion (or expected date of graduation), degree or certificate earned, and the institution's name and address. Include workshops, seminars, explorer programs, and related classes as well.
- *Skills*: Skills include computer literacy, leadership skills, organizational skills, or time-management skills. This is where you should also list certifications or licenses. Be specific in this area when possible.

- *Activities/Extracurriculars*: These can be related to skills such as an activity led to you developing a skill you listed. This section can be combined with the skills section, but it's helpful to break the sections apart if you have enough substantive things to say in both areas. Examples of activities and extracurriculars include sports, leadership roles, community service work, clubs and organizations, and so on.
- *Experience*: Here, in reverse chronological order, you should list the jobs you have worked in. The first one on your list may well be your current or recent apprenticeship. Don't worry if some of the jobs you've had don't seem particularly relevant to what you're applying for. Include them anyway and do your best to make them seem relevant. You're young, and it's understood that you haven't had a lot of time to gain direct experience in the field you're after. Of course, you should emphasize any jobs that are especially relevant. Here's where you can include part-time jobs, summer jobs, and volunteer experience.
- *Interests*: This section is optional, but it's a chance to include special talents and interests. Keep it short, factual, and specific. Show your passion for the field here.
- *References*: It's best to say that references are available on request. If you do list actual contacts, list no more than three and make sure you inform your contacts that they might be contacted.
- *Awards*: Honor roll or National Merit Scholarship information could be included here. The first three entries above are pretty much standard, but the other entries can be creatively combined or developed to maximize your abilities and experience. These are not set-in-stone sections that every resume must have. As an example, consider this mock functional resume, which uses a combination of these sections to accentuate Grace's strengths.

If you're still not seeing the big picture here, it's helpful to look at student and part-time resume examples online to see how others have approached this process. Search for "functional resume examples" to get a look at some examples.

Grace M. Edwards

1450 Audubon Circle
Stanley, OR, 97035
Phone: 503-503-5030 E-Mail: rec2020@student.com

Objective

To continue my passion in law enforcement by working in a probation office with experienced professionals and providing support and assistance to them.

Education

High School Diploma, June 2020
Westhaven High School, Stanley, OR

Included two criminal justice classes and three psychology classes

Skills

- Explorer Program Trained
- Use Windows and Mac suites proficiently
- CPR certified

- Excellent communication skills
- Organized and nonjudgmental

Key Achievements & Awards

Outstanding Community Service Award, 2019
Explorer Program graduate, Portland PD, 2018
Honor Roll, all four years

Professional Experience

August 2017-September 2019, Two years experience volunteering at the Aurora County Jail
June 2018-August 2018, Explorer Program, Portland PD, Portland, OR

References

Available upon request

A functional-style resume is a good template to use when you don't have a lot of work experience.

RESUME-WRITING TIPS

Regardless of your situation and why you're writing the resume, there are some basic tips and techniques you should use:

- Keep it short and simple. This includes using a simple, standard font and format. Using one of the resume templates provided by your word processing software can be a great way to start.

> **Note:** According to the job-search site Ladders (www.theladders.com), a recruiter spends an average of just six seconds reading each resume.[1]

- Use simple language. Keep it to one page.
- Highlight your academic achievements, such as a high grade point average (GPA) (above 3.5) or academic awards. If you have taken classes related to the job you're interviewing for, list those briefly as well.
- Emphasize your extracurricular activities, internships, etc. These could include clubs, sports, dog walking, babysitting, or volunteer work. Use these activities to show your skills and abilities.
- Use action verbs, such as led, created, taught, ran, and developed.
- Be specific and give examples.
- Always be honest.
- Include leadership roles and experience.
- Edit and proofread at least twice. Ask a professional (such as your school writing center or your local library services) to proofread it for you also. Don't forget to run spell check.
- Include a cover letter (discussed in the next section) unless specifically instructed not to.

Your final product should be simple and clear. Don't get caught up in choosing fancy typefaces, elaborate graphics or color schemes, or funky staggered paragraphs, or anything like that. Think about what the person reading the resumes wants. Above all, they want to save time. They don't want to be looking through resumes. It's not a fun job. It gets old very quickly. It tends to cause headaches. Make their job as easy as possible when they get to yours; they'll appreciate it.

Here are some final practical things to keep in mind when creating your resume:

- Save it in a few different formats so you have them all ready to go at any time. Most of the time you'll be uploading the resume online to companies, and the most common requested file formats are Microsoft Word, PDF, and plain text.
- Have several dozen printed out and handy, ready for you to give out at a moment's notice.
- Create customized versions for employers you're really interested in. If you're sending out twenty resumes and five of them are going to places where you'd be especially excited to work, create a special resume for each one of those five. Carefully study what kind of company/organization each one is, what skills and experience they are looking for, and make your resume to them reflect your best effort at being what they want.
- Highlight your accomplishments, not just the routine, day-to-day things you did in some past job. Anything in your experience you did that made you stand out from the crowd, make it prominent.

THE COVER LETTER

Every resume you send out usually includes a cover letter. This can be the most important part of your job search because it's often the first thing that potential employers read. By including the cover letter, you're showing the employers that you took the time to learn about their organization and address them personally. This goes a long way to show that you're interested in the position. See the sidebar called "Resumes, Cover Letters, and Online Job Applications" for exceptions to the standard cover letter approach. Sometimes the standard cover letter will be replaced by the body of the email you send.

Be sure to call the company/organization or verify on the website the name and title of the person to whom you should address the letter/email. This letter/email should be brief. Introduce yourself and begin with a statement that will grab the person's attention. Keep in mind that they will potentially receive hundreds of resumes and cover letters/emails for an open position. You want yours to stand out. Important information to supply includes:

- Your name, address, phone number, and email address
- The date
- The recipient's name, title, company name, and company address
- Salutation

Then you begin the letter portion of the cover letter or email, which should mention how you heard about the position, something extra about you that will interest the potential employer, practical skills you can bring to the position, and past experience related to the job. You should apply the facts outlined in your resume to the job to which you're applying. Each cover letter/email should be personalized for the position/company to which you're applying. Don't use "To Whom It May Concern." Instead, take the time to find out to whom you should actually address the letter.

Finally, end with a complimentary closing (also called a *salutation*), such as "Sincerely, Grace Edwards" and be sure to add your signature. Use "Mr." for male names and "Ms." for female names in your salutation. If you can't figure out the sex of the person who will be handling your application from their name, just use the full name ("Dear Jamie Smith").

Search online for "sample cover letters for internships" or "sample cover letters for high schoolers" to see some good examples. For more advice on cover letters, check out the free guide by Resume Genius at https://resumegenius .com/cover-letters-the-how-to-guide.

Your cover letter/email should be as short as possible while still conveying a sense of who you are and why you want this particular job or to work for this particular organization. Do your research on the organization and include some details about it in your letter/email—this demonstrates that you cared enough to take the time to learn something about them.

Finally, be sure to note all the specifications of each potential employer, especially when you are applying for a specific position. Some may not want you to include a cover letter at all; others may have specific instructions about formats and what kinds of information they expect you to include. Be sure to follow any of these instructions/requests very closely. It's your first (and maybe only) chance to show the potential employer that you can read instructions and follow directions correctly.

RESUMES, COVER LETTERS, AND
ONLINE JOB APPLICATIONS

Resumes and cover letters are holdovers from the era before the Internet—from before personal computers even. They were designed to be typed on paper and delivered through the mail. Obviously, nowadays much of the job application process has moved online. Nevertheless, the essential concepts communicated by the resume and cover letter haven't changed. Most employers who accept online applications either ask that you email or upload your resume.

Those who ask you to email your resume will specify which document formats they accept. The Adobe Acrobat PDF format is often preferred, because many programs can display a PDF (including web browsers), and documents in this format are mostly uneditable—that is, they can't easily be changed. In these cases, you attach the resume to your email, and your email itself becomes the "cover letter." The same principles of the cover letter discussed in this section apply to this email, except you skip the addresses and date at the top and begin directly with the salutation.

Some employers direct you to a section on their website where you can upload your resume. In these cases, it may not be obvious where your cover letter content should go. Look for a text box labeled something like "Personal Statement" or "Additional Information." Those are good places to add whatever you would normally write in a cover letter. If there doesn't seem to be a text box like that, see if there is an email link to the hiring manager or whoever will be reading your resume. Go ahead and send your "cover email" to this address, mentioning that you have uploaded your resume (again, omitting the addresses and date at the top of your cover letter). Use the person's name if it was given.

The goal of spending so much time and effort crafting a great resume and cover letter is to achieve one thing: an interview. It's the interview that will determine whether you get the job or not.

DEVELOPING YOUR INTERVIEWING SKILLS

The best way to avoid nerves and keep calm when you're interviewing is to be prepared. It's okay to feel scared, but keep it in perspective. It's likely that you'll receive many more rejections in your professional life than acceptances, as we all do. However, you only need one "yes" to start out. Think of the interviewing process as a learning experience. With the right attitude, you will learn from each experience and get better with each subsequent interview. That should be your overarching goal. Consider these tips and tricks when interviewing, whether it be for a job, internship, recruitment position, or something else entirely:[2]

- Practice interviewing with a friend or relative. Practicing will help calm your nerves and make you feel more prepared. Ask for specific feedback from your friends. Do you need to speak louder? Are you making enough eye contact? Are you actively listening when the other person is speaking?
- Learn as much as you can about the organization. Also be sure to understand the position for which you're applying. This will show the interviewer that you are motivated and interested in their organization.
- Speak up during the interview. Convey to the interviewer important points about you. Don't be afraid to ask questions. Try to remember the interviewers' names and call them by name.
- Arrive early and dress professionally and appropriately (you can read more about proper dress in a following section).
- Don't show up hungry or thirsty or having to go to the bathroom. Give yourself plenty of time to take care of that stuff before you arrive.
- Take some time to prepare answers to commonly asked questions. Be ready to describe your career or educational goals to the interviewer.

Common prompts/questions you may be given/asked during a job interview include:

- Tell me about yourself.
- What are your greatest strengths?
- What are your weaknesses?
- Tell me something about yourself that's not on your resume.
- What are your career goals?
- How do you handle failure? Are you willing to fail?
- How do you handle stress and pressure?

The interview might be with one person or more than one at the same time. © shironosov/iStock/ Getty Images

- What are you passionate about?
- Why do you want to work for us?

Tip: Bring a notebook and a pen to the interview. That way you can take some notes, and it'll give you something to do with your hands.

Jot down notes about your answers to these questions, but don't try to memorize the answers. You don't want to come off too rehearsed during the interview. Remember to be as specific and detailed as possible when answering these questions. Your goal is to set yourself apart in some way from the other people they will interview. Always accentuate the positive, even when you're asked about something you did not like, or about failure or stress. Most importantly, though, be yourself.

Tip: *Active listening* is the process of fully concentrating on what is being said, understanding it, and providing nonverbal cues and responses to the person talking.[3] It's the opposite of being distracted and thinking about something else when someone is talking. Active listening takes practice. You might find that your mind wanders and you need to bring it back to the person talking (and this could happen multiple times during one conversation). Practice this technique in regular conversations with friends and relatives. In addition to giving a better interview, it can cut down on nerves and make you more popular with friends and family, as everyone wants to feel that they are really being heard. For more on active listening, check out www.mindtools.com/CommSkll/ActiveListening.htm.

You should also be ready to ask questions of your interviewer. In a practical sense, there should be some questions that you have that you can't find the answer to on the website or in the literature. Also, asking questions shows that you are interested and have done your homework. Avoid asking questions about salary or special benefits at this stage, and don't ask about anything negative that you've heard about the company or school. Keep the questions positive and relative to you and the position to which you're applying. Some example questions to potential employers include:

- What is a typical career path for a person in this position?
- How would you describe the ideal candidate for this position?
- How is the department organized?
- What kind of responsibilities come with this job? (Don't ask this if they've already addressed this question in the job description or discussion.)
- What can I do as a follow-up?
- When do you expect to reach a decision?

Remember, it's a good idea to practice interviewing with a friend or relative. Or at least practice by yourself, answering common interview questions. The Balance Careers website (www.balancecareers.com) has a long list of common questions asked in interviews (https://www.thebalancecareers.com/job-interview-questions-and-answers-2061204). You could spend quite a while going through those questions and coming up with answers to prepare yourself.

When you're talking to the interviewer, relax. Take your time. Use as much detail as you can when describing your education and experience. Look the interviewer in the eye when you talk.

> **Tip:** If you know someone who already works at the company/organization, ask him or her for some inside advice and find out whether it's okay to mention his or her name during the interview. If the interviewer finds out you know someone who works there, that can really work in your favor.

DRESSING APPROPRIATELY

A job interview means you have to wear a suit and tie, right? Well, if you want to become a lawyer or judge, yes, but maybe not if you're interviewing for a job as a parole officer. A police chief or director might look at you funny if you show up dressed to the nines.

The look you're going for here is *business casual.* That means less formal than business attire, like a suit, but a step up from jeans, a t-shirt, and sneakers:

- *For men*: You can't go wrong with khaki pants, a polo or button up shirt, and brown or black shoes.
- *For women*: Nice slacks, a shirt or blouse that isn't too revealing, and nice flats or shoes with a heel that's not too high.

> **Tip:** You may want to find out in advance whether the organization has a dress code. Don't hesitate to ask the person who's going to interview you if you're unsure what to wear. You can also call the main number and ask the receptionist what people typically wear to interviews.

KNOWING WHAT EMPLOYERS EXPECT

You're almost certainly not the only candidate the employer is interviewing for the position. And if you think about it, they would only have called in people who were qualified for the job. That means, based on education, skills, and

Even something like "business casual" can be interpreted in many ways, so do some research to find out what exactly is expected of you. © PeopleImages/E+/Getty Images

experience, all the people who are interviewing could technically do the job. How, then, will they choose from all the candidates?

According to *Forbes* magazine, employers are looking for twelve qualities in you as an employee, and the interview process is meant to bring out these qualities for evaluation:[4]

- Work well on a team
- Understand your path
- Know what you want in your career
- Can point to your successes
- Know your strengths
- Think independently
- Like to problem solve
- Have ambition
- Are proactive
- Like learning new things
- Are goal-oriented
- Are responsible

Tip: Being able to convince an employer that you love to learn new things is one of the best ways to turn yourself into a candidate they won't be able to pass up. One last piece of advice, and in the end this may be the most valuable and crucial of all: *be the kind of person other people like working with.* It's sort of the Golden Rule as applied to the workplace.

TO SHAKE OR NOT TO SHAKE?

A handshake is a traditional form of greeting, especially in business. When you arrive for a job interview—or just meet someone new—a good firm handshake shows that you are a person to be taken seriously.

But shaking hands is not done in every culture, and even in North America, the norm of shaking hands has changed. During the COVID-19 crisis, people stopped shaking hands in order to avoid spreading germs. As things get back to normal, some people will want to resume shaking hands and some people won't. Maybe the whole culture around shaking hands will change permanently.

When you arrive for a job interview, follow the lead of the person you're meeting with. A respectful head nod or elbow bump is just fine, and probably safer.

Shaking hands in the 21st century is something to think about. © PeopleImages/E+/Getty Images

FOLLOWING UP

Be sure to follow up, whether via email or regular mail, with a thank you note to the interviewer. Following up is a delicate procedure that must be handled with a certain amount of thought and care. A good way to think of it is that you want to be on their mind but not in their face. You don't want to let too many days go by without any communication, but you also don't want to bug them or become annoying.

Following up usually takes place over the phone or through email. You want to follow up after these events (unless they contact you first):

- *After sending a resume/cover letter to a prospective employer*: If you promptly receive an email or phone call acknowledging your correspondence, that's probably good enough for now. You contacted them and they contacted you. You're even, and at that point you should give them around a week to contact you again. If they don't within a week, it's appropriate to contact them again (via the same method, phone or email) to inquire about setting up a time to meet and discuss the matter further. This shows you haven't forgotten and are still interested.

- *After submitting your application*: If you submitted a job application online, you will likely receive a confirmation email right away. If you mailed in your application, you may get a postcard a few days later to acknowledge it—or not. In either case, online or through the mail, if you hear nothing for a week, it's generally okay to contact them again to inquire about it. This shows you're eager for the job.

- *After being invited to an interview*: A short email to thank them for scheduling an interview is appropriate. This is simply to be polite.

- *After an interview*: Immediately after your interview, you *must* go home and compose an email to your interviewer or to your contact at the company who set up the interview (or to both—use your sense of what is appropriate). Do this as soon as possible. Within the hour if you can. In this email you should thank them for their time and for the opportunity to discuss the position. Say you enjoyed meeting them and look forward to talking with them again. This is also a matter of politeness, and it shows professionalism, respect, and courtesy.

Caution: Always read the instructions carefully regarding submitting an application or corresponding with a company. If they spell out rules for contacting them, *do not break those rules without a very good reason*. Wondering about how they liked your resume or when you'll be interviewed are not good enough reasons. The only good reason would be that you are no longer interested or available as a candidate (for example, because you just accepted another job).

EFFECTIVELY HANDLING STRESS

As you're forging ahead with you life plans, whether it's training camp, a full-time job, or even a gap year, you might find that these decisions feel very important and heavy and that the stress is difficult to deal with. First off, that's completely normal. Try these simple stress-relieving techniques:

- Take deep breaths in and out. Try this for thirty seconds. You'll be amazed at how it can help.
- Close your eyes and clear your mind.
- Go scream at the passing subway car. Or lock yourself in a closet and scream. Or scream into a pillow. For some people, this can really help.
- Keep the issue in perspective. Any decision you make now can be changed if it doesn't work out.

Want ways to avoid stress altogether? They are surprisingly simple. Of course, simple doesn't always mean easy, but it means they are basic and make sense with what we know about the human body:

- Get enough sleep.
- Eat healthy.
- Get exercise.
- Go outside.
- Schedule downtime.
- Connect with friends and family.

The bottom line is that you need to take time for self-care. There will always be conflict, but how you deal with it makes all the difference. This only becomes increasingly important as you enter the workforce and maybe have a family. Developing good, consistent habits related to self-care now will serve you all your life.

> *Beware the social media trap!* Prospective employers will check your social media sites, so make sure there is nothing too personal, explicit, or inappropriate on your sites. When you communicate out to the world in this way, don't use profanity, and be sure to use proper grammar. Think about the version of yourself you are portraying online. Is it favorable, or at least neutral, to potential employers? They will look, rest assured.

MATTHEW BROADNAX: WORKING WITH KIDS

Matthew Broadnax. Courtesy of Matthew Broadnax.

Master Patrol Officer Broadnax is a native of Detroit, Michigan, and attended high school in Bloomington, Indiana. He is a graduate of Indiana University, where he obtained his bachelor of science degree in exercise science in 1994, and his master of science degree in clinical exercise physiology in 1997. After graduate school, he worked in the health and fitness industry as a health fitness specialist, exercise physiologist, before finishing as a wellness director with the YMCA of Greater Indianapolis. After many years in his chosen profession, he decided to pursue a lifelong dream and accepted a position with the Indianapolis Public Schools Police Department (IPSPD) as a police officer (PO). After one and a half years with the IPSPD, he accepted a position with the Carmel Police Department as a patrolman. During his eleven years with the Carmel Police Department, he has been fortunate to have experience and training as a field evidence technician, as well as a field training officer. He is married, with three children, and is a diehard IU fan.

Can you explain how you became interested in being a police officer? Why an officer in the educational setting?

I am originally from Detroit and my uncle was a Detroit police officer for over forty years. I always admired him. Later in my career, I decided I really wanted to pursue a career in law enforcement.

I like helping people and enforcing rules, so I thought it was a good fit for my personality. I applied to the Indianapolis Public Schools (IPS) and the Carmel Police Department at the same time. I entered the police academy and worked for IPS and then was called by Carmel. I made a lateral change to Carmel and spent about eight years as a patrolman. But I loved working with kids at IPS. Occasionally, I would work at the high school and at the sporting events. Those experiences rekindled my love of being around kids. I waited for an open student resource officer (SRO) position and finally got in. I am currently in my fifth year as an SRO.

What's a "typical" day in your job?

I am the SRO at five schools in the district—one of the middle schools and its four feeder elementaries. I am responsible for law enforcement issues, mentoring, and education (typically in the form of presentations). I start my day at the middle school. I don't like to be predictable—I don't want to be a target or a victim. I build relationships with the kids as well as with the staff and parents. I serve the whole school community. I am at the elementary schools at least once per week, not including when I am called there for issues. I want to be part of every culture and part of the family at all five schools.

At the elementary, I might be called because we suspect a student is being abused or neglected. They said someone touched or hurt them, or they don't have enough food or clothing. Also, I am called for mentoring. A kid is struggling with homelife problems and they need someone to talk to.

At the middle school, it's less about abuse and neglect issues because they aren't willing to divulge issues they are having at home. We have social media drama issues and conflicts with other students. There are also school bullying issues and personal responsibility issues. My philosophy is—you are like my kids. Sometimes I yell at them with love, sometime I love them, but I always have high expectations for them.

What's the greatest challenge facing people working with juveniles in the justice system at this time?

Understanding the teen brain is a challenge—not everyone should be a police officer or work with kids. You have to understand them and know how they think and be empathetic to what they are dealing with and where they are coming from.

What's the best part of being in this field?

For me, it's all about building relationships. That gives me the most reward and satisfaction. Getting to know the kids—seeing them overcome challenges. I have known some of these kids since age one, and growing with them and being a constant in their lives is really rewarding.

What's the most challenging part of being a resource officer?

Working with kids whose brains aren't done developing. They don't always make good decisions. I work with lots of kids who make the same mistakes again and again. You are trying to guide them to make better choices. You want to help them make fewer mistakes.

Do you think your time at the academy adequately prepared you for your job?

As an SRO, not really. Acting as a police officer in the school setting, it did prepare me. My specialized training for being an SRO from the National Association for SROs—they have training, contacts, and conferences. You get training that way. We have a great partnership between the city and the school system, too, which helps.

Where do you see the field of criminal justice going in the future?

It's becoming more tenuous for law enforcement and that can hurt recruitment. How we are perceived in the community can put up walls and make the job difficult. I've seen an erosion of respect for first responders of all kinds during my time as a PO. I think the push for SRO in all schools is very beneficial, but it has to be done the right way. The right person has to be there—someone who likes children and wants to be around children. I've met some over the years who don't like children—not good for a school setting! They can do more harm than good.

What traits or skills make for a good SRO?

You need to have patience, a good sense of humor, be a good listener, be empathetic, and be a good role model—outside and in your job.

What advice do you have for young people considering this career?

Do it for the right reasons. Make sure it's a good fit for you and your personality. You should find joy in it or don't do it.

How can a young person prepare for a career in criminal justice while in high school?

Look for Police Explorer programs, which are for young people ages thirteen to twenty-one, usually. You can shadow and learn what they do. Most SROs are advisors for our program. Attendees get a uniform and we have a rank structure. They get training and education about what POs do. They can go on ride-alongs once they are eighteen. The Carmel Police Teen Academy for ages thirteen through eighteen is a summer program and a mini-police academy. You learn about fitness, firearms, defensive tactics, and get to tour the jail. You also get to interact with police officers on a more personal basis. Find the programs in your town and try them out.

Tip: *Personal contacts can make the difference!* Don't be afraid to contact people you know. Personal connections can be a great way to find jobs and internship opportunities. Your high school teachers, your coaches and mentors, and your friends' parents are all examples of people who very well may know about jobs or internships that would suit you. Start asking several months before you hope to start a job or internship, because it will take some time to do research and arrange interviews. You can also use social media in your search. LinkedIn, for example, includes lots of searchable information on local companies. Follow and interact with people on social media to get their attention. Just remember to act professionally and communicate with proper grammar, just as you would in person.

Summary

This chapter covered writing your resume and cover letter, applying for jobs online, and polishing your interviewing skills. You learned the vital importance of communication, both written and verbal, to a successful job search. And you discovered tips and tricks that should serve you long into your career.

Well, you made it to the end of this book! Hopefully you have learned enough about these fields to start along your journey, or to continue with your path. If you've reached the end and you feel like one of these careers is right for you, that's great news. Or, if you've figured out that this isn't the right field for you, that's good information to learn too. For many of us, figuring out what we *don't* want to do and what we *don't* like is an important step in finding the right career.

With a little hard work and perseverance, you'll be on your way to career success! © FlamingoImages/ iStock/Getty Images

There is a lot of good news about a career in criminal justice. It's a great career for people who get energy from working with other people. Job demand is steady and will continue to grow. Whether you decide to attend a four-year university, go to community college, or take a gap year, having a plan and an idea about your future can help guide your decisions. We hope that by reading this book you are well on your way to having a plan for your future. Good luck to you as you move ahead!

Notes

Introduction

1. Dictionary.com, "Criminal Justice," n.d., https://www.dictionary.com/browse/criminal-justice.

2. CorrectionalOfficerEDU.org, "What is a Correctional Officer?" n.d., https://www.correctionalofficeredu.org/what-is-a-correctional-officer/.

3. CareerExplorer.com, "What Does a Probation Officer Do?" August 29, 2020, https://www.careerexplorer.com/careers/probation-officer/.

4. Bureau of Labor Statistics, US Department of Labor, *Occupational Outlook Handbook* (hereafter referred to as BLS, *OOH*), "Summary" (tab 1) on the "Police and Detectives" webpage, last updated September 1, 2020, https://www.bls.gov/ooh/protective-service/police-and-detectives.htm.

5. BLS, *OOH*, "Summary" (tab 1) on the "Probation Officers and Correctional Treatment Specialists" webpage, last updated September 1, 2020, https://www.bls.gov/ooh/community-and-social-service/probation-officers-and-correctional-treatment-specialists.htm.

6. BLS, *OOH*, "Summary" (tab 1) on the "Security Guards and Gambling Surveillance Officers" webpage, last updated September 30, 2020, https://www.bls.gov/ooh/protective-service/security-guards.htm.

7. BLS, *OOH*, "Summary" (tab 1) on the "Judges and Hearing Officers" webpage, last updated September 1, 2020, https://www.bls.gov/ooh/legal/judges-and-hearing-officers.htm.

8. BLS, *OOH*, "Summary" (tab 1) on the "Lawyers" webpage, last updated September 1, 2020, https://www.bls.gov/ooh/legal/lawyers.htm.

Chapter 1

1. CollegeAtlas.org, "Statistics of a College Dropout," https://www.collegeatlas.org/wp-content/uploads/2014/08/college-dropout-2017.jpg.

2. Adapted from Bureau of Labor Statistics, US Department of Labor, *Occupational Outlook Handbook* (hereafter referred to as BLS, *OOH*), "What Police and Detectives Do" (tab 2) on the "Police and Detectives" webpage, last updated September 1, 2020, https://www.bls.gov/ooh/protective-service/police-and-detectives.htm#tab-2.

3. BLS, *OOH*, "Summary" (tab 1) on the "Police and Detectives" webpage, last updated September 1, 2020, https://www.bls.gov/ooh/protective-service/police-and-detectives.htm.

4. Ibid.

5. BLS, *OOH,* "Summary" (tab 1) on the "Probation Officers and Correctional Treatment Specialists" webpage, last updated September 1, 2020, https://www.bls.gov/ooh/community-and-social-service/probation-officers-and-correctional-treatment-specialists.htm#tab-1.

6. BLS, *OOH*, "What Probation Officers and Correctional Treatment Specialists Do" (tab 2) on the "Probation Officers and Correctional Treatment Specialists" webpage, last updated September 1, 2020, https://www.bls.gov/ooh/community-and-social-service/probation-officers-and-correctional-treatment-specialists.htm#tab-2.

7. CareerExplorer.com, "What Does a Probation Officer Do?" August 29, 2020, https://www.careerexplorer.com/careers/probation-officer/.

8. BLS, *OOH*, "What Police and Detectives Do" (tab 2) on the "Police and Detectives" webpage, last updated September 1, 2020, https://www.bls.gov/ooh/protective-service/police-and-detectives.htm#tab-2.

9. BLS, *OOH*, "Summary" (tab 1) on the "Probation Officers and Correctional Treatment Specialists" webpage, last updated September 1, 2020, https://www.bls.gov/ooh/community-and-social-service/probation-officers-and-correctional-treatment-specialists.htm#tab-1.

10. Ibid.

11. BLS, *OOH*, "What Correctional Officers and Bailiffs Do" (tab 2) on the "Correctional Officers and Bailiffs" webpage, last updated September 1, 2020, https://www.bls.gov/ooh/protective-service/correctional-officers.htm#tab-2.

12. Christina Bush, "Pros and Cons of Being a Correctional Officer," Career Trend, December 8, 2018, https://careertrend.com/info-8353723-pros-cons-being-correctional-officer.html.

13. *Chron* Contributor, "The Advantages of a Career as a Corrections Officer," *Chron*, June 17, 2020, https://work.chron.com/advantages-career-corrections-officer-15094.html. https://work.chron.com/advantages-career-corrections-officer-15094.html.

14. S. Konda, H. Tiesman, A. Reichard, and D. Hartley, "US Correctional Officers Killed or Injured on the Job," *Corrections Today* 75, no. 5 (2013): 122–23. https://www.ncbi.nlm.nih.gov/pmc/articles/PMC4699466/.

15. BLS, *OOH*, "Job Outlook" (tab 6) on the "Correctional Officers and Bailiffs" webpage, last updated September 1, 2020, https://www.bls.gov/ooh/protective-service/correctional-officers.htm#tab-6.

16. BLS, *OOH*, "Summary" (tab 1) on the "Correctional Officers and Bailiffs" webpage, last updated September 1, 2020, https://www.bls.gov/ooh/protective-service/correctional-officers.htm#tab-1.

17. BLS, *OOH*, "What Security Guards and Gambling Surveillance Officers Do" (tab 2) on the "Security Guards and Gambling Surveillance Officers" webpage, last updated September 30, 2020, https://www.bls.gov/ooh/protective-service/security-guards.htm#tab-2.

18. Deggy, "Risks of Security Guards," company blog, posted on April 4, 2018, https://www.deggy.com/post-risks-of-security-guards.html.

19. BLS, *OOH*, "Job Outlook" (tab 6) on the "Security Guards and Gambling Surveillance Officers" webpage, last updated September 30, https://www.bls.gov/ooh/protective-service/security-guards.htm#tab-6.

20. BLS, *OOH*, "Summary" (tab 1) on the "Security Guards and Gambling Surveillance Officers" webpage, last updated September 30, https://www.bls.gov/ooh/protective-service/security-guards.htm#tab-1.

21. Laura Reynolds, "The Role of Judges in Criminal Cases," *Chron*, August 29, 2020, https://work.chron.com/role-judges-criminal-cases-6696.html.

22. Jason Silverstein, "Which States Still Have the Death Penalty?" *CBS News*, March 14, 2019, https://www.cbsnews.com/news/which-states-still-have-the-death-penalty/.

23. BLS, *OOH*, "Summary" (tab 1) on the "Judges and Hearing Officers" webpage, last updated September 1, 2020, https://www.bls.gov/ooh/legal/judges-and-hearing-officers.htm#tab-1.

Chapter 2

1. SecurityGuard-License.org, "How to Become a Security Guard: Starting Out," August 29, 2020, https://securityguard-license.org/articles/how-to-become-a-security-guard.html.

2. Bureau of Labor Statistics, US Department of Labor, *Occupational Outlook Handbook*, "How to Become One" (tab 4) on the "Security Guards and Gambling Surveillance Officers" webpage, last updated September 30, https://www.bls.gov/ooh/protective-service/security-guards.htm#tab-4.

3. *Chron* Contributor, "The Advantages of a Career as a Corrections Officer," *Chron*, June 17, 2020, https://work.chron.com/advantages-career-corrections-officer -15094.html.

4. All Criminal Justice Schools, "Learn About Probation Officer Careers," Corrections Degrees and Careers, n.d.,https://www.allcriminaljusticeschools.com/ corrections/career-probation-officer/.

5. Lou Adler, "New Survey Reveals 85% of All Jobs Are Filled via Networking," LinkedIn, September 12, 2020, https://www.linkedin.com/pulse/new-survey-reveals -85-all-jobs-filled-via-networking-lou-adler/.

Chapter 3

1. Peter Van Buskirk, "Finding a Good College Fit," *US News & World Report*, June 13, 2011, https://www.usnews.com/education/blogs/the-college-admissions -insider/2011/06/13/finding-a-good-college-fit.

2. National Center for Education Statistics, "Fast Facts: Graduation Rates," August 22, 2020, https://nces.ed.gov/fastfacts/display.asp?id=40.

3. Attributed to Benjamin Franklin, Poor Richard, in The Home Book of Quo- tations, ed. Burton Stevenson, 10th ed., p. 1054 (1967), and in The Home Book of American Quotations, ed. Bruce Bohle, p. 220 (1967). Reported as unverified in Respectfully Quoted: A Dictionary of Quotations (1989).

4. Discover Policing, "Basic Requirements," August 20, 2020, https://www .discoverpolicing.org/about-policing/basic-requirements/.

5. Study.com, "Correction Officer: How Do I Become a Correctional Offi- cer?" March 3, 2020, https://study.com/articles/Correction_Officer_How_Do_I_ Become_a_Correctional_Officer.html.

6. Neumann, Rita, "LSAT Scores for the Top 100 Law Schools: Good LSAT Scores, Bad LSAT Scores, and Acceptable LSAT Scores," *Magoosh LSAT* Blog, October 14, 2016, https://magoosh.com/lsat/2016/lsat-scores-top-100-law-schools/.

7. Ibid.

8. Ilana Kowarski, "See the Price, Payoff of Law School Before Enrolling," *US News & World Report*, March 18, 2020, https://www.usnews.com/education/best -graduate-schools/top-law-schools/articles/law-school-cost-starting-salary.

9. Ibid.

10. Ibid.

11. Farran Powell and Emma Kerr, "What You Need to Know About College Tuition Costs," *US News & World Report*, September 17, 2020, https://www.usnews

.com/education/best-colleges/paying-for-college/articles/what-you-need-to-know-about -college-tuition-costs.

12. College Board, "For Parents and Guardians: How Much is Tuition?" n.d., https://parents.collegeboard.org/faq/how-much-tuition.

13. Justin Boyle, "How Much Does Trade School Costs?" Real Work Matters, September 10, 2019, https://www.rwm.org/articles/how-much-does-trade-school-cost/.

14. College Board, "Understanding College Costs," August 20, 2020, https://bigfuture.collegeboard.org/pay-for-college/college-costs/understanding-college-costs.

15. Ibid.

16. Gap Year Association, "Research Statement," September 12, 2020, https://gapyearassociation.org/.

17. Federal Student Aid. "FAFSA Changes for 2017–2018." August 12, 2020. https://studentaid.ed.gov/sa/about/announcements/fafsa-changes.

Chapter 4

1. The Ladders, "Keeping an Eye on Recruiter Behavior," August 15, 2020, https://cdn.theladders.net/static/images/basicSite/pdfs/TheLadders-EyeTracking-StudyC2.pdf.

2. Justin Ross Muchnick, Teens' Guide to College and Career Planning, 12th ed. (Lawrenceville, NJ: Peterson's Publishing, 2015), 179–80.

3. Mind Tools, "Active Listening: Hear What People Are Really Saying," August 29, 2020, https://www.mindtools.com/CommSkll/ActiveListening.htm.

4. Liz Ryan, "12 Qualities Employers Look for When They're Hiring," Forbes, March 2, 2016, https://www.forbes.com/sites/lizryan/2016/03/02/12-qualities -employers-look-for-when-theyre-hiring/#8ba06d22c242.

Glossary

1. American Bar Association, "How Court Works," September 9, 2019, https://www.americanbar.org/groups/public_education/resources/law_related_education_network/how_courts_work/motions/.

Glossary

accreditation: The act of officially recognizing an organizational body, person, or educational facility as having a particular status or being qualified to perform a particular activity. For example, schools and colleges are accredited. See also *certification*.

ACT: The American College Test (ACT) is one of the standardized college entrance tests that anyone wanting to enter undergraduate studies in the United States should take. It measures knowledge and skills in mathematics, English, reading, and science reasoning, as they apply to college readiness. There are four multiple-choice sections. There is also an optional writing test. The total score of the ACT is 36. See also *SAT, LSAT*.

active listening: The process of fully concentrating on what is being said, understanding it, and providing nonverbal cues and responses to the person talking. It's the opposite of being distracted and thinking about something else when someone is talking to you.

associate's degree: A degree awarded by community or junior colleges that typically requires two years of study.

bachelor's degree: An undergraduate degree awarded by colleges and universities that is typically a four-year course of study, when pursued full-time, but this can vary by degree earned and by the university awarding the degree.

bar association/the bar: This is a professional group of qualified lawyers (collectively known as "the bar," or "members of the bar"). The word *bar* is derived from the old English/European custom of using a physical railing to separate the area in which court business is done from the viewing area for the general public.

certification: The action or process of confirming certain skills or knowledge of a person. Usually provided by some third-party review, assessment, or educational body. Individuals, not organizations, are certified. See also *accreditation*.

detective unit: These police officers gather facts and collect evidence for criminal cases. They conduct interviews, examine records, observe the activities of suspects, and participate in raids and arrests. Detectives usually specialize in investigating one type of crime, such as homicide or fraud. They can be uniformed or plainclothes investigators.

gap year: A gap year is a year between high school and college (or sometimes between college and post-graduate studies) whereby the student is not in school but is instead, typically, involved in volunteer programs, such as the Peace Corps, in travel experiences, or in work and teaching experiences.

grants: Money to pay for postsecondary education that is usually awarded to students who have financial need but can also be awarded in the areas of athletics, academics, demographics, veteran support, and special talents. Grants do not have to be paid back.

internal affairs unit: These police officers investigate and unearth what really occurred when an officer or department is accused of misconduct. They ordinarily work outside of the traditional command structure.

LSAT: The Law School Admission Test (LSAT) is a standardized test in the United States that anyone applying to law school must take. It's a half-day test given in two parts. The first part is composed of multiple-choice questions and the second part is an essay. It is intended to complement a student's undergraduate GPA in determining readiness for law school. The total score of the LSAT is 180. See also *ACT, SAT.*

master's degree: A secondary degree awarded by colleges and universities that requires at least one additional year of study after obtaining a bachelor's degree. The degree holder shows mastery of a specific field.

motion (in court): This is a procedural device used to bring a limited, contested issue before a court for decision. It is a request to the judge (or judges) to make a decision about the case. Two of the more common pretrial motions are *motions to discover*—when one party wants pertinent information from the opposing party—and *motions to dismiss*—where the judge is asked to dismiss the lawsuit because it isn't legally sound, even if all the facts alleged are proven true.[1]

personal statement: A written description of a person's accomplishments, outlook, interest, goals, and personality that's an important part of a college application. The personal statement should set an applicant apart from others. The required length depends on the institution, but generally ranges from one to two pages, or five hundred to a thousand words.

parole: Conditional freedom for a prison inmate. The parolee is released from prison but has to live up to a series of responsibilities. A parolee who doesn't follow the rules risks going back into custody. See also *parolee.*

parolee: A convicted criminal who has been released from jail and must follow certain guidelines and rules, including regularly reporting to a parole officer for a period of time specified by the parole board. See also *parole.*

postsecondary degree: A degree above and beyond a high school education. This is a general description that includes trade certificates and certifications, associate's degrees, bachelor's degrees, master's degrees, and beyond.

probationer: Someone who was arrested and found guilty of a crime but is allowed to stay out of prison if they do not commit another crime and follow particular rules during the probationary period.

PTSD: post-traumatic stress disorder (PTSD) is an anxiety disorder that can be the result of experiencing a traumatic event. People suffering from PTSD may have intense fear, helplessness, guilt, and stress long after an event is over. They often relive these events in their mind and suffer from flashbacks. Many first responders struggle with bouts of PTSD due to the traumatic nature of their jobs.

SAT: The Scholastic Aptitude Test (SAT) is one of the standardized tests in the United States that anyone applying to undergraduate studies should take. It measures verbal and mathematical reasoning abilities as they relate to predicting successful performance in college. It is intended to complement a student's GPA and school record in assessing readiness for college. The total score of the SAT is 1600. See also *ACT, LSAT.*

scholarships: Merit-based aid used to pay for postsecondary education that does not have to be paid back. Scholarships are typically awarded based on academic excellence or some other special talent, such as music or art.

statute of limitations: A law that forbids prosecutors from charging someone with a crime that was committed more than a specified number of years earlier. Also referred to as *time limits,* these statutes can put pressure on criminal justice professionals to effectively charge, try, and close cases in an expedient manner. Certain crimes, like murder and kidnapping, do not have a statute of limitations.

SWAT unit: The Special Weapons and Tactics (SWAT) team is an elite unit within a police force used for exceptional crisis situations that require increased firepower or special tactics. They often deal with hostage and terrorist situations, for example.

vice unit: These police officers focus on crime related to narcotics, alcohol, gambling, and prostitution. Sometimes these officers go "undercover" to investigate a potential illegal operation.

Further Resources

Are you looking for more information about the fields under the criminal justice umbrella, which in this book include police officers, parole/probation officers, correctional officers, and criminal court prosecutors/judges? Do you want to know more about the application process or need some help finding the right educational/vocational fit for you? Do you want a quick way to search for a good college or school? Try these resources as a starting point on your journey toward finding a great career!

Books

Fiske, Edward. *Fiske Guide to Colleges.* Naperville, IL: Sourcebooks, 2018.

Franek, Robert. *The Best 382 Colleges, 2018 Edition: Everything You Need to Make the Right College Choice.* New York: Princeton Review, 2018.

Gilmartin, Kevin M. *Emotional Survival for Law Enforcement: A Guide for Officers and Their Families.* E-S Press, 2002.

Muchnick, Justin Ross. *Teens' Guide to College and Career Planning.* 12th ed. Lawrenceville, NJ: Peterson's Publishing, 2015.

Strock, James. *Serve to Lead 2.0: Twenty-First Century Leaders Manual.* 2nd ed. Scotts Valley, CA: CreateSpace, 2018.

Titus, Alfred S., Jr. *The Personal Side of Policing: An In-Depth Look at How a Career in Law Enforcement Can Change and Affect Your Life.* Valley Stream, NY: A. Titus Consulting, 2018.

Websites

American Bar Association
www.americanbar.org

The American Bar Association's mission is "to serve equally our members, our profession and the public by defending liberty and delivering justice as the national representative of the legal profession." Membership includes access to a job board, free continuing education opportunities, career webinars, articles and podcasts, connections to other lawyers, and more.

American Gap Year Association

www.gapyearassociation.org

The American Gap Year Association's mission is "making transformative gap years an accessible option for all high school graduates." A gap year is a year taken between high school and college to travel, teach, work, volunteer, generally mature, and otherwise experience the world. Their website has lots of advice and resources for anyone considering taking a gap year.

The Balance

www.thebalance.com

This site is all about managing money and finances but also has a large section called "Your Career," which provides advice for writing resumes and cover letters, interviewing, and more. Search this site for "teens" and you can find teen-specific advice and tips.

The College Board

www.collegeboard.org

The College Entrance Examination Board tracks and summarizes financial data from colleges and universities all over the United States. This site can be your one-stop shop for all things college research. It contains lots of advice and information about taking and doing well on the SAT and ACT, many articles on college planning, a robust college-search feature, a scholarship-search feature, and a major- and career-search area. You can type your career of interest (for example, occupational therapy) into the search box and get back a full page that describes the career and gives advice on how to prepare, where to get experience, how to pay for it, what characteristics you should have to excel in this career, lists of helpful classes to take while in high school, and lots of links for more information. It's a great, well-organized site.

College Grad Career Profile

www.collegegrad.com/careers

Although this site is primarily geared toward college graduates, the careers profile area (indicated in the link above) has a list of links to nearly every career you could ever think of. A single click takes you to a very detailed, helpful section that describes the job in detail; explains the educational requirements; includes links to good colleges that offer this career and links to actual open jobs and internships; describes the licensing requirements, if any; lists salaries; and much more.

Kahn Academy

www.khanacademy.org

The Kahn Academy website is an impressive collection of articles, courses, and videos about many educational topics in math, science, and the humanities. You can search any topic or subject (by subject matter and grade) and read lessons, take courses, or watch videos to learn all about it. The site includes test prep information for the SAT, ACT, AP, GMAT, and other standardized tests. There is also a "College Admissions" tab with lots of good articles and information, provided in the approachable Kahn style.

Live Career

www.livecareer.com

This site has an impressive number of resources directed toward teens, for writing resumes, cover letters, and interviewing.

Mapping Your Future

www.mappingyourfuture.org

This site helps young people figure out what they want to do and maps out how to reach career goals. It includes helpful tips on resume writing, job hunting, job interviewing, and more.

Monster

www.monster.com

Perhaps the most well-known and certainly one of the largest employment websites in the United States. Fill in a couple of search boxes and away you go.

You can sort by job title, of course, as well as by company name, location, salary range, experience range, and much more. The site also includes information about career fairs, advice on resumes and interviewing, and more.

Bureau of Labor Statistics
www.bls.gov
The Bureau of Labor Statistics unit of the US Department of Labor produces this website. It offers lots of relevant and updated information about various careers, including average salaries, how to work in an industry, a job's outlook in the job market, typical work environments, and what workers do on the job. See www.bls.gov/emp/ for a full list of employment projections.

Peterson's College Prep
www.petersons.com
In addition to lots of information about preparing for the ACT and SAT and easily searchable information about scholarships nationwide, Peterson's site includes a comprehensive search feature to search for universities and schools based on location, major, name, and more.

Police1
www.police1.com
Dubbed as "the one resource for police officers and law enforcement," this site includes news from all of the country, training advice, and videos of all things related to law enforcement. You can find breaking news, product reviews, job postings, and more.

Police Magazine
www.policemag.com
A magazine dedicated to providing law enforcement officers of all ranks with information that will help them do their jobs more efficiently, professionally, and safely. Each issue of Police includes columns written by current and retired police, firearms, and legal experts, as well as topical, issue-oriented features produced by leading law enforcement journalists.

Law Officer

www.lawofficer.com

This site provides law enforcement with daily breaking news stories, as well as editorials about the tactics, technology, and training they need to stay safe on the job.

Study.com

www.study.com

This is a site similar to Kahn Academy, where you can search any topic or subject and read lessons, take courses, and watch videos to learn all about it.

TeenLife: College Preparation

www.teenlife.com

This organization calls itself "the leading source for college preparation," and it includes lots of information about summer programs, gap-year programs, community service, and more. TeenLife believes that spending time "in the world" outside of the classroom can help students develop important life skills. This site contains lots of links to volunteer and summer programs.

***US News & World Report*: College Rankings**

www.usnews.com/best-colleges

US News & World Report provides almost fifty different types of numerical rankings and lists of colleges throughout the United States to help students with their college search. You can search colleges by best reviewed, best value for the money, best liberal arts schools, best schools for "B" students, and more.

Bibliography

Adler, Lou. "New Survey Reveals 85% of All Jobs Are Filled via Networking." LinkedIn. September 12, 2020. https://www.linkedin.com/pulse/new -survey-reveals-85-all-jobs-filled-via-networking-lou-adler/.

All Criminal Justice Schools. "Learn About Probation Officer Careers." Corrections Degrees and Careers. n.d. https://www.allcriminaljusticeschools .com/corrections/career-probation-officer/.

American Bar Association. "How Court Works." September 9, 2019. https:// www.americanbar.org/groups/public_education/resources/law_related_ education_network/how_courts_work/motions/.

Boyle, Justin. "How Much Does Trade School Costs?" Real Work Matters. September 10, 2019. https://www.rwm.org/articles/how-much-does-trade -school-cost/.

Bureau of Labor Statistics, US Department of Labor, *Occupational Outlook Handbook*, last modified September 2020. https://www.bls.gov/ooh.

Bush, Christina. "Pros and Cons of Being a Correctional Officer." Career Trend. December 18, 2018. https://careertrend.com/info-8353723-pros-cons -being-correctional-officer.html.

CareerExplorer. "What Does a Probation Officer Do?" August 29, 2020. https://www.careerexplorer.com/careers/probation-officer.

Chron Contributor. "The Advantages of a Career as a Corrections Officer." *Chron.* June 17, 2020. https://work.chron.com/advantages-career -corrections-officer-15094.html.

CollegeAtlas.org. "Statistics of a College Dropout." n.d. https://www.college atlas.org/wp-content/uploads/2014/08/college-dropout-2017.jpg.

CollegeBoard. "For Parents and Guardians: How Much is Tuition?" n.d. https://parents.collegeboard.org/faq/how-much-tuition.

CollegeBoard. "Understanding College Costs." Big Future. August 20, 2020. https://bigfuture.collegeboard.org/pay-for-college/college-costs/under standing-college-costs.

CareerExplorer.com. "What Does a Probation Officer Do?" August 29, 2020. https://www.careerexplorer.com/careers/probation-officer/.

Common Core State Standards Initiative. "Preparing American's Students for Success." August 18, 2020. http://www.corestandards.org.

CorrectionalOfficerEDU.org. "What is a Correctional Officer?" n.d. https://www.correctionalofficeredu.org/what-is-a-correctional-officer/.

Deggy, "Risks of Security Guards." Company blog. Posted April 4, 2018. https://www.deggy.com/post-risks-of-security-guards.html.

Dictionary.com. "Criminal Justice." https://www.dictionary.com/browse/criminal-justice.

Discover Policing. "Basic Requirements." August 20, 2020. https://www.discoverpolicing.org/about-policing/basic-requirements/.

Federal Student Aid. "Learn What's New with the FAFSA Process." December 12, 2020. https://financialaidtoolkit.ed.gov/tk/learn/fafsa/updates.jsp.

Federal Student Aid. "FAFSA Changes for 2017–2018." August 12, 2020. https://studentaid.ed.gov/sa/about/announcements/fafsa-changes.

Fiske, Edward. *Fiske Guide to Colleges.* Naperville, IL: Sourcebooks, 2018.

Gap Year Association. "Research Statement." September 12, 2020. https://gapyearassociation.org/.

GoCollege. "Types of Scholarships." September 12, 2020. http://www.gocollege.com/financial-aid/scholarships/types/.

Keates, Cathy. "What Is Job Shadowing?" TalentEgg. September 9, 2020. https://talentegg.ca/incubator/2011/02/03/what-is-job-shadowing/.

Konda, S., H. Tiesman, A. Reichard, and D. Hartley. "US Correctional Officers Killed or Injured on the Job." *Corrections Today* 75, no. 5 (2013): 122–23. https://www.ncbi.nlm.nih.gov/pmc/articles/PMC4699466/.

Kowarski, Ilana. "See the Price, Payoff of Law School Before Enrolling." March 18, 2020. *US News & World Report.* https://www.usnews.com/education/best-graduate-schools/top-law-schools/articles/law-school-cost-starting-salary.

The Ladders. "Keeping an Eye on Recruiter Behavior." August 15, 2020. https://cdn.theladders.net/static/images/basicSite/pdfs/TheLadders-EyeTracking-StudyC2.pdf.

McKay, Dawn Rosenberg. "Career Choices," The Balance Careers. April 24, 2018. https://www.thebalance.com/career-choice-or-change-4161891.

Mind Tools. "Active Listening: Hear What People Are Really Saying." August 29, 2020. https://www.mindtools.com/CommSkll/ActiveListening.htm.

Muchnick, Justin Ross. *Teens' Guide to College and Career Planning.* 12th ed. Lawrenceville, NJ: Peterson's Publishing, 2015.

National Center for Education Statistics. "Fast Facts: Graduation Rates." August 22, 2020. https://nces.ed.gov/fastfacts/display.asp?id=40.

National Center for Education Statistics. "Private School Enrollment." January 2018. https://nces.ed.gov/programs/coe/indicator_cgc.asp.

Neumann, Rita. "LSAT Scores for the Top 100 Law Schools: Good LSAT Scores, Bad LSAT Scores, and Acceptable LSAT Scores." October 14, 2016. *Magoosh* LSAT Blog. https://magoosh.com/lsat/2016/lsat-scores-top-100-law-schools/.

Powell, Farran, and Emma Kerr. "What You Need to Know About College Tuition Costs." September 17, 2020. *US News & World Report.* https://www.usnews.com/education/best-colleges/paying-for-college/articles/what-you-need-to-know-about-college-tuition-costs.

Reynolds, Laura. "The Role of Judges in Criminal Cases," *Chron.* August 29, 2020. https://work.chron.com/role-judges-criminal-cases-6696.html.

Ryan, Liz. "12 Qualities Employers Look for When They're Hiring." *Forbes,* March 2, 2016. https://www.forbes.com/sites/lizryan/2016/03/02/12-qualities-employers-look-for-when-theyre-hiring/#8ba06d22c242.

SecurityGuard-License.org. "How to Become a Security Guard: Starting Out." August 29, 2020. https://securityguard-license.org/articles/how-to-become-a-security-guard.html.

Silverstein, Jason. "Which States Still Have the Death Penalty?" *CBS News.* March 14, 2019. https://www.cbsnews.com/news/which-states-still-have-the-death-penalty/.

Study.com. "Correction Officer: How Do I Become a Correctional Officer?" March 3, 2020. https://study.com/articles/Correction_Officer_How_Do_I_Become_a_Correctional_Officer.html.

US Department of Education. "Fact Sheet: Focusing Higher Education on Student Success." July 27, 2015. https://www.ed.gov/news/press-releases/fact-sheet-focusing-higher-education-student-success.

Van Buskirk, Peter. "Finding a Good College Fit." *US News & World Report.* June 13, 2011. https://www.usnews.com/education/blogs/the-college-admissions-insider/2011/06/13/finding-a-good-college-fit.

About the Author

Kezia Endsley is an editor and author from Indianapolis, Indiana. In addition to editing technical publications and writing books for teens, she enjoys running and triathlons, traveling, reading, and spending time with her family and many pets.

CPSIA information can be obtained
at www.ICGtesting.com
Printed in the USA
LVHW011719030521
686332LV00005BB/588